PARTNERS
IN
EVERYTHING

PARTNERS IN EVERYTHING

Your Couples' Guide

To Running a Successful Business

Without Ruining Your Life

Hank and Sharyn Yuloff

with

Kati and Alex Pauls

and

Star and Mark Tomlinson

Naked Book Publishing

PUBLISHED BY Naked Book Publishing

Paperback ISBN 978-0-986-0888-7-2

DISCLAIMER AND/OR LEGAL NOTICES
While all attempts have been made to verify information provided in this book and its ancillary materials, neither the author or publisher assumes any responsibility for errors, inaccuracies or omissions and is not responsible for any financial loss by customer in any manner. Any slights of people or organizations are unintentional. If advice concerning legal, financial, accounting or related matters is needed, the services of a qualified professional should be sought. This book and its associated ancillary materials, including verbal and written training, is not intended for use as a source of legal, financial, or accounting advice. You should be aware of the various laws governing business transactions or other business practices in your particular geographical locations.

EARNINGS & INCOME DISCLAIMER
With respect to the reliability, accuracy, timeliness, usefulness, adequacy, completeness, and/or suitability of information provided in this book, Henry "Hank" Yuloff, Sharyn Yuloff, Naked Book Publishing, its partners, associates, affiliates, consultants, and/or presenters make no warranties, guarantees, representations, or claims of any kind. Readers' results will vary depending on a number of factors. Any and all claims or representations as to income earnings are not to be considered average earnings. Testimonials are not representative. This book and all products and services are for educational and informational purposes only. Use caution and see the advice of qualified professionals. Check with your accountant, attorney or professional advisor before acting on this or any information. You agree that Henry "Hank" Yuloff, Sharyn Yuloff and/or Naked Book Publishing are not responsible for the success or failure of your personal, business, health or financial decisions related to any information presented by Henry "Hank" Yuloff, Sharyn Yuloff, Naked Book Publishing or company products or services. Earnings potential is entirely dependent on the efforts, skills, and application of the individual person.

Any examples, stories, references, or case studies are for illustrative purposes only and should not be interpreted as testimonies and/or examples of what reader and/or consumers can generally expect from the information. No representation in any part of this information materials and/or seminar training are guarantees or promises for actual performance. Any statements, strategies, concepts, techniques, exercises and ideas in the information, materials and/or seminar training offered are simply opinion or experience, and thus should not be misinterpreted as promises, typical results or guarantees (expressed or implied). The author and publisher (Henry "Hank" Yuloff, Sharyn Yuloff, Naked Book Publishing nor any of their representatives) shall in no way, under any circumstances, be held liable to any party (or third party) for any direct, indirect, punitive, special, incidental or other consequential damages arising directly or indirectly from any use of books, materials and/or seminar trainings, which is provided "as is," and without warranties.

PRINTED IN THE UNITED STATES OF AMERICA

Here's to thirty years!

Contents

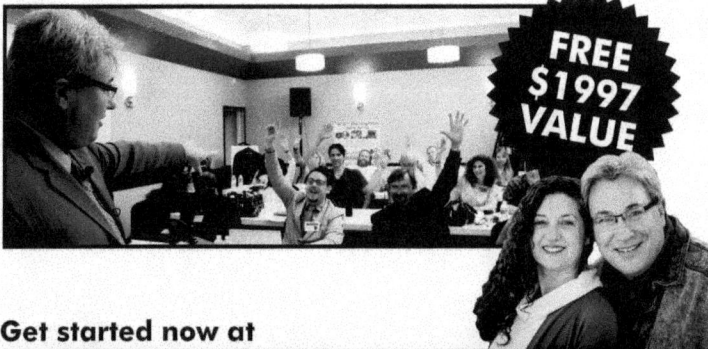

Acknowledgments

Dan Janal—who gave us the idea of writing this book. We vividly remember the meeting in Los Angeles when you told us that "you two should write a book about couples working together." His giving attitude made a positive change in our business and is a perfect example of the power of the mastermind process. Dan, thank you for being the spark!

We want to thank our editor, *Terri Boekhoff.* This is our 7th book together. She has made each of them better . . . and we get to take the credit. Knowing that "Terri will be reading this" has made us far more confident in our writing. We cannot possibly fully express how grateful we are to have her as a member of our team. We wish all writers the joy that comes from having an editor like Terri. Can we do one more? Maybe two?

Sharone Rosen—who introduced us. My G-d, what would our lives be without you?

James Malinchak and Cindy McLane—a brother and sister partner team, that taught us a lot about running our business together. They each have a lane and give the other the freedom to make their business a smooth-running machine!

John Limbocker—Our SEO oracle and the go-to guy for all things online. This man is a genius.

Forbes Riley—reminded us how important we think it is to live in integrity. Never TRY—always DO. Remember to surrender to the process.

Deborah & Glen—We firmly believe that marriages are easier when your family believes in you. We are grateful that you have always supported us and encouraged us in all our efforts. We look forward to more decades supporting each other together!

Hank's Parents—The pain we feel missing you will never go away but the things you taught us are an everyday reminder of the right way to do things. They were Hank's example in every way on how to be *partners in everything*.

Our clients—Y'all are our reason to stay on top of what's going on in sales, marketing, HR, and small business. Because of you we know we must stay sharp. We will never betray the trust you have put in us. Thank you for trusting us to help you build your business.

About the Cover

Thanks to everyone who gave us input on our cover art–a very close vote.

This cover took a quite different path than the covers of all our other books. Mostly because there were so many voices quoted here, we felt that a photo of us on the cover would not serve it justice. *Early* in the process of discussing *Partners In Everything*, we found a piece of clip art that was a woman and man on a teeter totter. That was going to be the model of a photograph of us. Did you know, that it is rather difficult, impossible even, to find a teeter totter on a playground? We searched for a place to reproduce that clip art with us on the teeter totter. Finally, it became clear that a graphic was the only way to go instead of the photo.

And since we have had to constantly answer the question "why is Sharyn up above Hank instead of you two being even?" here is the answer—it's the physics of it. Hank weighs a bit more than Sharyn. With gravity doing what it does, when we both sit on a teeter totter, he goes down, and she goes up. To capture that moment in time when we happened to be level with each other would make for a difficult drawing. You feel it when you see it. Something is . . . wrong because our bodies would be in what looked like extremely uncomfortable positions. There's that, and when we were drawn in this position, valuable real estate was gained on the cover for the subtitle.

Here is a bonus tidbit: We had five drawings created for this cover—two of which were competing for the final. Since we could not decide, we have saved the other one for our next marketing tips book, *The Marketing Checklist 3, Even 49 MORE Simple Ways to Master Your Marketing*. Look for it soon!

Foreword

You may remember me from being featured on the hit ABC TV show, "Secret Millionaire." If you do not know of the show, here is the basic premise from show promotions:

"What happens when business motivational speaker and self-made millionaire James Malinchak is picked up by an ABC television crew, placed on an airplane with no money, credit cards, cell phone, laptop or watch, and is whisked off to an impoverished neighborhood, where he had to survive on $44.66 cents for a week?

The show features Malinchak leaving his current lifestyle in search of real-life heroes who are making a difference in their local community. He ultimately reveals himself as a millionaire and rewards them with a portion of his own money to further their cause by gifting them with checks of his own money totaling over $100,000. If you watched ABC's 'Secret Millionaire' you know that James is no ordinary entrepreneur. He is a self-made millionaire with a strong passion for giving back and serving others."

Amazingly, over 50 MIILLION people watched the show!

Whether I am speaking at a conference, walking through an airport, consulting for an entrepreneur or just hanging out at a coffee shop, I always seem to get asked the same question. "What was it like being on Secret Millionaire when you had to live undercover and how did it affect you?"

My answer is always the same.

The greatest gift you can have is when you simply give in order to help and serve others. There is no better feeling than when you know you have made a positive difference in lives of others.

And that is *exactly* what Sharyn and Hank and their wisdom, teachings and life experiences can do for you! Sharyn and Hank truly care about making a positive difference in the lives of others.

Some strategies may comfort you while others may challenge your old paradigm. One thing is for certain, Sharyn and Hank will stamp your spirit with an abundance of knowledge and encouragement.

It is my sincere honor to introduce to you to Sharyn and Hank and their book!

James Malinchak
Featured on ABCs Hit TV Show, *"Secret Millionaire"*
Authored 25 Books, Delivered 3,000 Presentations &
2,000 Consultations
The World's Leading Speaker Trainer & Coach
Founder, www.BigMoneySpeaker.com

Preface

The idea for this book came to us at a mastermind meeting when Dan Janal said we should write a book about couples working together "because you do it so well."

As we thought about writing the book, and discussed it, and brooded on it, the obvious decision was that unlike our other books, we could not write this book alone. We are exceptionally good at running our successful business without ruining our lives, however, we did not feel that our system was the only way to do it.

We found two couples to be co-authors. They run their businesses much differently than we do. You will hear from us and these two other sets of partners in the first section. We sent all the couples a set of fifteen questions on how they manage their partnership. Our section illustrates the questions that we asked.

We also found another nine couples to interview on their point of view (they got the same questions). It will give you an idea of how different partner couples each handle a particular issue.

You'll find author information for everyone at the back of the book.

And, as the publication date is our thirtieth wedding anniversary, we felt we needed to leave you with some relationship wisdom—from us and others—to help you on your way.

Because we are small business coaches and teaching is what we do, we have also added a bonus essay on marketing to help you build your business. And as you see from the cover of the book, when you go to *FreeVIPBonus. com* there is a bonus online free video training section with an action guide for you.

Thank you for investing in your business by reading *Partners In Everything*. We look forward to hearing from you on how it has helped you. Perhaps we will invite you to appear on our podcast, The Marketing Checklist View Cast. You can reach us at info@YuloffCreative.com.

Introduction—This Is How We Do It and These Are the Lessons You Will Learn

Scene: Office interior. 3:06 a.m. Unable to sleep because of Entrepreneur's Brain, Hank, sitting at his desk, Word Doc open, new file, blinking cursor. For dramatic effect he puts on "This Is How We Do It" by Montell Jordan.

Well, here we go again. For the seventh time, we have committed ourselves to writing a book. But this one is different. Instead of putting marketing first, this one begins with couples who are in business together, then building the business together, and then marketing.

This book is written by business owners who rather than going solo, have taken on a partner to run it together. Sometimes partners are romantically connected. Sometimes it's a parent-child partnership or siblings. This connection brings with it extra challenges to go along with the extra brain power to make the business successful. It's that second set of eyes that can view everything from a different point of view that we know gives us a unique advantage in the world of business.

For example, I know that in about an hour, I will have a couple thousand words behind me. I don't do a whole lot of editing as I write because I know that I have a safety net—Sharyn. This is how we do 75% of our writing. I take the first pass at the subject of choice, and she will be the first person to see these words and with the red pen of an editor, will go through the work and make it reflect both of us. After her first pass, I am the first editor. That's why when you read our other books and the blogs on YuloffCreative.com that are the basis for most of our books, you hear predominantly one of our voices or the other, but we usually don't tell you who it is. But this book is different. This book is written primarily for other couples in business together and we want to give you a road map for how you might make things better.

1

This does not mean that we do not have unique challenges, which might offset that extra brain power.

In college, I worked for three family-run companies and that was my introduction into a type of business that had both challenges and blessings. I worked for a pharmacy (husband and wife) and two ticket agencies (one was two brothers and a cousin, the other the tricky husband-wife-father-in-law-mother-in-law-brother combination). In minutes, they could go from smooth as a mountain lake at dawn, to a level four hurricane.

In the business world, working for someone else, I had countless retail and service businesses as clients for my direct mail, promotional product, and advertising jobs. Sharyn and I have also worked with a lot of family-owned businesses and find that the challenges they face are exciting for us to work with.

It is for all you small business owners in partnership that we, and several other couples, wrote this book.

That is another reason this book is different. You won't just hear our voices as you read it. And that takes a bit longer to write. Let's rephrase that: it took a lot longer to prepare, to write, and coordinate it.

It was several years ago, now, when the idea for this book came to us. Actually, the idea was *delivered* to us.

In his book, *Think and Grow Rich*, Napoleon Hill wrote about the power of masterminding. That is where several like-minded people come together to solve their mutual challenges. In this case, we were in James Malinchak's mastermind for small business owners, mostly from the United States. We gathered a few times a year for two days each time to look at various facets of our businesses.

Interestingly, though I always came home with many pages of notes, the best idea we came away from that particular two-day event was this book. *First lesson of this book*: It isn't always what happens in the room that is important. And it did not happen during a session. At the end of day one, Dan Janal and I exchanged books. He gave me *Write Your Book in a Flash* and I gave him our latest book, *The Marketing Checklist 2: 49 MORE Ways to Master Your Marketing*. Dan's business is helping people write and promote their first book. And he is good at it.

The next morning, Dan came up to me and said he loved our book. He said it was great. "You know, you and Sharyn should write a book about working together."

(Pause. Cursor blinking on mental page for about three seconds.)

I'm forever grateful that I was in mastermind mode, which means, I was in accept-information-from-the-universe mode. In those three seconds I went from, "now that would be a silly book" to "wow . . . couples that work together *are* one of our target audiences . . . we *must* write a book about couples working together."

Second lesson of this book: We, you and I, do not have the market cornered on good ideas. Be open to accepting information and more information will forever flow towards you.

If you are big on history, you grabbed your copy *of The Marketing Checklist 2* and checked the copyright date and saw 2016. And then checked the copyright of *this* book and saw 2021.

If you are a fan of *Think and Grow Rich*, you also know that he talks about taking massive action on an idea to bring it to fruition. Sharyn and I are usually quite good at that. But things happen. We had our *Small Business Human Resources* (2017) book to finish, *The Hows and Whys of Social Media* (2018) and *The Marketing Checklist for Sales* (2019) books already on the white board. And, we had another book on physics and marketing on that same board and . . . . I didn't say we *always* take massive action, but in our defense, it wasn't like we have not been creating content. Right now, I could pull enough content from our hard drives to write *The Marketing Checklist 3: Another 49 Ways to Master Your Marketing*.

But this book has been percolating. And percolating. We had the cover concept three years ago after I found a piece of clipart of a couple sitting on a seesaw. We knew we would take a photo of us on that playground device. Parenthetically, it's impossible to *find* one when you want one and then it must be the right size, so we ended up with the current version.

So how did we decide that *now* is the time? The pandemic. We had been on a roll of a book a year for six years and then, well, you know what happened in 2020.

During that year, we pivoted our business. Lots of live events turned into teleconference virtual events. Our time on the road turned into office time. And that begged the continuous question . . .

"How are other couples managing this shit?"

Clearly it was time to write it. Our motto in 2020 was "get comfortable being uncomfortable!" In 2021 it became "if it doesn't bring us joy, we're not doing it!"

Here's the thing that I began several paragraphs ago—this is not just our voice. One of the things that slowed down the process of this book was that we knew we did not want to write it by ourselves. How Sharyn and I run our business is different than how other couples run theirs. And you, dear reader, need to hear other solutions besides ours. So, as we began the running conversation (that lasted four years), we knew that we had to bring others into the process. And that stopped us in our tracks. We did what we help our clients avoid every day: Putting a roadblock in our way.

It turns out that getting others to buy into being part of a book is hard. We *knew* that going in because we know that being the author of several books puts us in an exceedingly small portion of the population. Heck, even the number of businesspeople who have written *one* book, *their* book, is small. We sent the proposal for this book to *dozens* of couples who raised their hand and said they had an interest in being interviewed.

Third lesson of this book: We forgot that the first rule of marketing is to give your prospects just enough information to get the right people to raise their hand and ask for more information. *Then* the sales process can proceed.

It seems that the same reason that keeps most people from writing a book is that they think that they can't write a book. Even being interviewed for a book is a daunting task for too many people. Now we were searching for a small subset of business owners, people who are partners in everything that own a business together that wanted to be part of the writing process, and it became a challenge.

And then the universe stepped in. In March 2021, I was on Clubhouse in a room doing a sixty-second pitch. I was looking for an introduction to people who were in business together to be interviewed for this book. And in the middle of my pitch (which was written down word for word) my sub-conscious took over.

The unscripted words popped out " . . . and as a way to celebrate twenty-five years in business together, and even more years in love, on July 21, our thirtieth wedding anniversary, we will publish the book."

Oh crap. I now had a deadline. Self-imposed for sure, but a deadline, nonetheless. And it was a sales pitch for the book when we went to press.

Let's go back to *Think and Grow Rich* and a hundred other self-improvement books: When you have a goal, if you add a date when it must be finished, it is more certain to happen.

Lesson four of this book: If you previously did not believe in that last paragraph and what it says, start.

Of course! Virtually every other book we had published had a deadline of one sort or another. My first book, *49 Stupid Things People do with Business Cards . . . And How to Fix Them* had to be finished and printed by a specific date because if it was, I got to speak to an audience of 250 business owners. It was the same type of thing for the next one, *The Marketing Checklist: 80*

Ways to Master Your Marketing. Another deadline, another completed book.

And if you have come to our Small Business Breakthrough Bootcamps (SBBB) you have heard the story of how *The Marketing Checklist for Sales* came about when we talk about mindset and goals.

(By the way, *lesson five of the book* just happened—I used a neuro linguistic programming technique to make you ask yourself the questions, "Well, what *is* that story?" and, "What is the SBBB?" and hopefully, FOMO (fear of missing out) kicks in and you might decide you want to attend one of them. We sent your subconscious mind on a quest. Want to know how to do that? Come to bootcamp. The information is at TheMarketingEvent.com.

So, we now had a deadline. Which means we sprang into action. And we found twelve couples to be interviewed. What this means for you is that you will hear several voices in this book, not just ours. Sharyn and I have *still* not cornered the market on how to do this right.

We sent a set of questions to these authors to gather information on certain angles of partnership. Two of the couples—Kati and Alex Pauls, and Star and Mark Tomlinson—have given us a more in-depth perspective of the way they manage being partners in everything to complement what we have wanted to share with you. That will be found in the first section of the book. The other nine have informed discussions on the subjects and you'll find them in the second section.

Lesson six of this book: That's how it works. Move forward, trust yourself. Trust the system. Trust in the universe. When you are open and in receive-mode, it will happen for you.

Oh, and if you are a believer in manifesting things we now add *lesson seven of this book*: Every time someone says that they are going to manifest something, Sharyn and I look at each other. Manifestation is great, but you know what makes manifestation even faster? Doing the work.

Not everyone picks their romantic partner thinking that they will go into business together. And people do not become friends with someone based on opening a company one day. When we were approached with the idea to write a book about "how being a successful couple in today's business climate is good for our clients," we jumped at the thought, and thought it would be an even more powerful book if we included other couples, who have learned to successfully and profitably work together.

In *Partners In Everything* we looked for couples to share their stories on how working together has challenged them, worked for them, and how their partnership has been beneficial for their clients.

This book isn't just for traditional couples—it is written for any two people who have taken the leap into business together and want to do it profitably.

Here's how the book works: Section one will begin with our partner experience. We used the questions that we first asked ourselves (and then asked the other partners) as *our* chapter headings so you can see what information we were seeking on partnerships. Our part of the book will be followed by that of Kati and Alex Pauls, then Star and Mark Tomlinson. Section two will be a subject discussion from nine more couples. Section three will have thirty tips on partnering (wonder how we came up with that number?). After our epilogue because Sharyn and I have *marketing A.D.D.*, we have added a bonus marketing chapter to help you build your business.

Let's get started. And just in case you need it, here is the best email address to connect with us: Info@YuloffCreative.com and here is the best link to get on our calendar: HowToGetThereFaster.com.

End scene: 4:06 a.m. Word count: 1842. With editing, that will be up over 2,200. Close file. Back to bed. Entrepreneur Brain satisfied.

Section One

Three Strong Partnerships

Hank and Sharyn Yuloff
Yuloff Creative Marketing Solutions

With over three decades in the business of helping entrepreneurs grow, survive and thrive, Sharyn and Hank Yuloff are small business coaches that remove road blocks that keep you from reaching your dreams.

1

Describe Your Business
and What Sets You Apart

If everything happens for a reason, be the reason things happen.
— Sharyn and Hank Yuloff

Let me share a story about my very first experience confronting the reality that small business owners were often taught how *to do* what they do, but not how *to market* what they do.

I had just begun working for my college newspaper, selling advertising space. On a cold call I went into the very first Subway sandwich shop in California, not knowing it was a franchise. After the owner explained that there would soon be a bunch of these shops in our town, he said that other than some possible ads, the company was leaving his advertising programs entirely up to him, and he was confused by it. He was, he said, a sandwich guy not a marketing guy.

I struggled with the idea that these *adults* (I was barely twenty years old) had no real concept about marketing and were looking to *me*, an advertising *student* to guide the company that they had invested their life savings to open. How was that possible? And he was not an outlier. I had a few dozen accounts that were completely looking to me to save their livelihoods. And I could not let them down.

It was during the two years of selling for, and then running the advertising department that I realized I had focused my dream of helping small business owners. I had a talent for it and following that dream would help thousands of families have a better life.

Move ahead many years and we're known as *America's #1 Coaching Team for Small Business Marketing* because we've taught thousands of small business owners the keys to successfully market and promote their companies.

To do that we had to create the business coaching program that we had always wanted for ourselves. After trying to work with half a dozen coaches and being ultimately disappointed, we finally created the program that we had been seeking.

To support those programs, we've published six best-selling business books, spoken on stages all over America, and coach small business owners to prosperity that they'd only dreamed of achieving.

Now, through webinars, seminars, and two-on-you coaching, we're helping small business owners like you understand the three keys to getting what you want from your business.

Sharyn grew up watching her grandparents run their own profitable business together. That taught her that couples can work side by side.

Hank grew up watching his parents work overtime for others while running a small business on the side. That's how they reached their dream of becoming millionaires and they shared that drive to overcome obstacles with him.

Our mission is to be the masters of our client's marketing message. We deliver their message directly to the eyes of their customer. Through superior coaching, our clients stay out of the habit of being in the habit.

We believe that when your business exists to serve your life, you will always be reminded to begin with the end in mind when marketing your business.

Small business owners that are good at what they do deserve a marketing plan that will increase their relevancy and raise their profits. We've created programs that make a positive difference to each client. The small business owners that join our group coaching program are taught that they can overcome a competitor who has more marketing dollars because they have been taught how to use a laser-like message.

We are the coaching team small business owners can turn to when they need their marketing questions answered honestly and accurately. We continuously offer a much better than expected value for a fair investment. We are the hand holders. We look for clients who know that they are the best at what they do, but just need some help telling the world.

We are your enemies of average which leads to our slogan:

If you want assistance in figuring out how your business is different and how to market it, connect with us at HowToGetThereFaster.com for your free thirty-minute success call.

2

Describe Your Relationship

*The only difference between stumbling blocks and stepping stones
is the way you use them.*

It began when Hank asked the cantor at his temple, "Who's the really cute woman in the brown pants that sat in the third row tonight?" Actually, it was a far more colorful question, and Sharone Rosen did her job as a member of the clergy and introduced two single adults.

If you ask us separately about our first date, you will get different answers, but we do agree on one thing. When we are asked, "How long have you been married," Hank has only one answer.

"Not long enough."

We often ask a coaching client what they want their life to look like. That's because our goal has always been to make our business serve *our* life instead of our life serving our business.

That's how we ended up in Sedona. When Hank's mother passed away, his dad had a bunch of time share weeks that he gladly let us use. We used seven weeks in six years to visit the town and decided that we could do our small business coaching from Arizona as easily as we had in Los Angeles.

Thinking

For the year prior to our wedding, we went to a marriage and family counselor, mostly to work on communication challenges. It seems that we each wanted to make certain that we were being heard by the other. And that was causing distress because evidently, we were not.

Leslie, our counselor, shared two lessons with us that have carried forward to this day.

When you are asked a question by your partner, sometimes you need a moment to form a response. Sometimes you don't hear the question at all.

The answer was, and still is, that if you hear the question and need a moment, you say, "thinking." That lets the other person know that they were heard.

If you don't get an answer or the word *thinking*, your question was lost to the ether, and you need to repeat it. Sometimes the radio just drowns us out.

That one action eliminated most of our arguments. And Sharyn even brought that into each office she worked in prior to us teaming up. It eliminated a lot of her frustrations.

The second lesson is a bit of politeness. When one of us walks into the other's work area with a question or thought, we begin with "are you interruptible?"

That's because we don't know if our partner in everything is in the middle of writing something to a client, for a client, or creating content. We don't want to interrupt their flow. 90% of the time the answer is, "Yes, what's up?" but those other times, we accept the "no" without attaching any value judgements. We are not being rejected; we just need a moment.

The other half of that is that as soon as our partner is done, they must immediately go to find out what is needed.

Describing our perfect day is easier when we remember that the main thing is to filter everything through the *does-it-bring-us joy* filter:

- Wake up without an alarm.
- Enjoy a (snog and a) leisurely breakfast.
- Pack a snack and head out for a hike (no more than two hours).
- Return home for a shower (or a swim) and lunch (maybe a nap).
- Answer emails.
- Enjoy dinner and a movie (or TV).
- Head to bed.

We see our life heading more and more in this direction as we have pivoted our business and only accepted the kinds of clients that we are able to put through that same filter.

If you want assistance in figuring out how to make your business serve your life instead of your life serving your business, connect with us at How-ToGetThereFaster.com for your free thirty-minute success call.

3

Tell Us about Your Average Work Schedule

This subject is one of the reasons we are writing this book. Creating balance is not one of our strong suits. We described our business as being the private and group coaching plans that we wished we could have found—because no matter how much we invested, we always ended up being disappointed.

So . . . we work.

A lot.

Client needs something. Client has a deadline. Client needs some prospects interviewed. Client needs a logo. Client has a question.

We're on it.

The work week is generally filled with client work, client calls, webinars to fill the top of our sales funnels, follow ups, and projects to promote our business.

Clearly life/work balance is something we are working to achieve. To that end, our plan is to pivot our business to take fewer two-on-you clients for private coaching and more clients in our group coaching programs.

There are a few days a year that we cannot be reached. There *are* a few days a year that we cannot be reached. Our Anniversary is always a top *us-only* day plus a few holidays and most Sundays.

When we are on vacation, we figured out a while ago that we can check email in the morning and the late afternoon and that seems to be fine.

Speaking of email—we *clearly* check ours far more often than most people. We are reminded of that each time that we hold the Small Business Breakthrough Bootcamp after we send out reminders for start times, and what they will learn, and how to be best prepared to get the most out of their experience.

Seasonally our business does not follow the normal winter, spring, summer, or fall. Here are ours:

Bootcamp Season: which happens between two absolute definite times in

March and September but can also occur in June and early December.

Book Season: When we publish a book, our entire public-facing marketing changes for a short period of time. We move from all content emails and posts having a "here is some free information to help you build your business" frame of reference to a "if you invest ninety-nine cents for our book, you get this really cool package of stuff" frame of reference.

On Boarding New Client Season: Bootcamp season is quickly followed by this season because after bootcamps we always have new members of our group coaching program who each receive a two-hour session.

Holiday Season: Interestingly, some years, the November/December holiday period is slow. Clients are on holiday, and no one seems to want to book their time. Attendance on our Monday mastermind calls dwindle. Other years, we cannot keep up with the traffic. *Everyone* wants to book time. Our promotional product business explodes with holiday gift orders. We can hardly come up for air. Also, interestingly, we have never been able to see a pattern between these two types of holiday seasons. We gear up for both.

Vacation Season: We love vacation season. It comes a couple of times a year when we can take a break. One of our favorite things to do is follow our baseball team, the Boston Red Sox (don't hate!) when they go on road trips. This has gotten us to Chicago and San Francisco (the first time the Sox played at Wrigley and by the bay), Seattle a few times, San Diego, and Washington DC for extended weekends.

In 2019 we followed them to the United Kingdom when they played a (horrible) pair of games against the Yankees. That was great because Sharyn has family in London and in the south of France, so we extended our trip a bit and enjoyed having Sharyn's brother, Scott join us.

By far, our favorite vacation seasons are when we can get on a cruise ship. That is where we can unplug the most and our "only check email twice a day" rule comes in handy. We have been on almost twenty cruises together that went to China, Tahiti, the Caribbean, New England (for the fall colors), and Mexico. We have finished two of our books sitting on a secluded part of the stern of a ship, laptops open, enjoying various beverages as we write.

We have taught continuing education courses on ships for organizations, and we have one of our own Education at Sea cruises planned for the end of this book's publication year where we have invited our clients to join us for special courses and fun.

Vacation season is definitely a break. Sometimes it can be a one-day event where we have decided that we need to recharge and spend the day connecting. How do you use *your* vacation days? Are they filled with *busy*? Or are they filled with *relax*?

4

What Do You Think of the Term Power Couple?

According to Dictionary.com, the term *power couple* is defined as "a romantic or married couple where both members are famous or accomplished in their own right, sometimes extended to happy and productive everyday couples."

There was an interesting article on that site about PCs— saying that the term began to supplant *super couple* in the 1980s. Bob and Elizabeth Dole (U.S. Senator and Secretary of Education, respectively) were one of the first. Madonna and Sean Penn, Phylicia and Ahmad Rashad, Paul and Linda McCartney (really? Linda?) were all given that label.

Eventually the term dribbled down from the famous and powerful to be used for local couples that everyone knew.

We have been called this term. For the record, we do not consider ourselves a power couple. We are a couple in business who are completely in love and have built a very successful business together. We are so connected that when one of us shows up at a gathering, it is just assumed that the other is also on hand.

We think the term is so overused that it has become a horrible cliché.

Just like when people call us *marketing gurus* when they want to say something nice about what we do but are not quite sure what to say about us.

For the record, we are not gurus.

Marketing oracles, yes, but gurus, no.

If you want assistance in figuring out how to teach people how to describe your business to your best benefit, talk to us.

5

Describe Your Office and Physical Space

For Sharyn, it was not until joining Hank in Yuloff Creative over a decade ago, that she had a home office. It has not been that way for Hank for a long time.

In January, 1987, Hank got a job with a promotional product company that did not have a local office in Los Angeles. Since then, he has worked at home. From an apartment in Tarzana, California, to an apartment in North Hollywood, to a condominium back in Tarzana, to houses in Reseda, Encino, and then Sedona, his office has been in his home.

In the last three homes, the garage was mostly used for sample storage for our promotional products business.

In the first two homes, one bedroom was used as an office.

When we bought our home in Sedona, it was bought with a specific purpose in mind. The living room is our war room where we work with clients. The walls are lined with white boards that allow for sketching out a client's marketing path.

What would have traditionally been the dining room is our office. That means that our office has incredible views.

Rounding out most of the bottom floor of the Sedona home, was a bonus room between the garage and the kitchen which has become a sound baffled audio and video studio complete with various lighting set ups.

If you want assistance in figuring out how your business can better use your workspace, connect with us at HowToGetThereFaster.com for your free thirty-minute success call.

6

Did Your Home Become a Second Office?

Not even close—our home is our main office.

If you look at our websites and business cards you will see an address that we use for our mail and package delivery. It has been the most logical thing for us to do for the past decade. The disappointing thing is that we did not do it years earlier.

When you work in the promotional product industry you get a lot of mail. Catalogs, random sample packages, invoices (yes, we still get printed invoices), and specials. What that means is that when we changed addresses, there was a lot of mail that fell through the cracks, and we did not get.

Our strongest recommendation for any business owner who is home-based is to use a mail drop address.

Our business style determined how we bought our last three homes. In Reseda, we bought a three bedroom so that there would be an office. In Encino, we bought a home that was going to need a bedroom added so that there would be an office. That was not a pleasant experience for us so when we moved to Sedona, Arizona, we were looking for a home that would be *business ready*.

So our current home has two levels. The upper level is a bedroom, and a guest room. The downstairs has a guest suite that we have used for clients (it has a separate entrance), the living room that is our work room for group meetings and client visits, and a dining room that, since we are not "gather in the dining room for a meal" people it is our office. When we looked for homes, this was what we were looking for. We can shut off the work area if we wish.

All of this to save the costs of a commercial office space because we do not shut things down at 5 p.m. or at dinner time. In fact, as this is being written, it's after 9 p.m., we are watching television and getting ready to head to bed.

In other words, a normal Tuesday evening.

We once figured out how much money we had saved by not having a commercial space since beginning Yuloff Creative.

At $2,000 a month, that would be $24,000 a year, and for 25 years, that is $600,000.

At $3,000 a month, that would be $36,000 a year, and for 25 years, that is $900,000.

All that revenue gone. And we would still take work home each night so why would we ever work any other way?

If you want assistance in figuring out how to better use your home as your work space, and some rules to make your home office more effective, connect with us at HowToGetThereFaster.com for your free thirty-minute success call.

7

How Did You Become Work Partners?

There are two specific days/stories/events that brought our business into focus. The first was a holiday.

Our company began inauspiciously. When going around the Thanksgiving table, sharing what we were thankful for, my mom noticed that I was not very happy being one of the sales managers for a national company.

I told her I was not. That there were several things which made the job a *job* instead of a career. I told her that there was less and less client contact, and that was what I was best at—helping businesses get more business. She looked at me with a look I was very familiar with—the let's-fix-this-now look. And she asked an awfully specific question: "What would it take for you to open your own business?"

I took a moment and realized that the only thing I would really need is a fax machine, since the one I had belonged to the company, and I would have to return it. I had everything else but a name.

Mom turned to my dad and said, "Write him a check," and then looked at me and said, "Come up with a name." It is those specific moments which we think back on that changed the direction of our lives and are so special.

That was over twenty-five years ago. In that time, Promotionally Minded, the name I chose from a long list, has grown in its marketing offerings from promotional products to small marketing projects, to advice on public relations, to complete marketing plans where often we are the ad-hoc marketing department for small companies under our own TheCompanyMarketing-Plan.com product name.

It has not been without growing pains—a couple of recessions and a *learning moment* or three has cost us dearly, but those setbacks and delays have also made us smarter and a better advisor to our clients. In fact, each time we have gone from business cruise control to business expansion, we have had the feeling that all entrepreneurs have: Time to just jump out of the nest and fly.

The best jump happened when Sharyn joined the company.

While recovering from a work-related injury, I got to eaves drop on conversations Hank was having with his clients. Even though I thought he was *the marketing guy* and I was just *HR and office management*, I realized that the conversations he was having with his clients were the same kinds of conversations I was having in my office. It was then we realized that HR is *internal marketing*. I was working with clients to hone their message to attract their supervisor, or colleagues, to their point of view. Or I was working with management to hone their messaging to attract the employees to adopt management's point of view.

After a year on disability, one of Hank's clients contracted us both to help with her small business because she needed help with her sub-contractors (HR and back-office systems a.k.a. Sharyn's forte), as well as identifying her ideal clients and packaging her services to them (marketing and sales, Hank's forte).

When that contract was over, we decided to continue working together with other clients and have never looked back!

The latest jump, and the biggest one by far, was the creation of the Small Business Breakthrough Bootcamps. We have always told our clients that being in a *category of one* was the way to move yourself up the Success Pyramid, and for us, this was a definite trailblazing experience. The excitement of taking all we have learned and keep learning in an ever-changing technological setting and sharing it all in small groups of entrepreneurs is exhilarating. The business owners who find us are true experts in their fields, and it is our job to help them deftly overcome competitors who either have had a marketing head start or, in some cases, are just flat outspending them. One client said that we approach our objectives like "marketing tornados with a David vs. Goliath chip on our shoulders."

When we do them in person, we put your marketing plan together for you in two and a half days. (When we do them virtually, we get it done in three days, for just three hours a day). We have widely expanded the programs to create comprehensive marketing plans for our attendees. We do them in Los Angeles and Phoenix and Sedona. If you're reading this, we invite you to experience the kind of marketing intensive bootcamp which will not only reenergize you, but it will reenergize your *sales*, will make your head spin with incredible marketing ideas and send you out as a new Goliath in your marketplace. And what really makes this over the top the coolest thing ever, is that if you come to Sedona for the bootcamp, it all takes place in a resort area that my Mom would have called "the kind of place reserved for people who appreciate how beautiful the Earth can be."

Your free ticket is at PlanYourMarketing.com.

Do you want to learn how to share your origin story so that it best promotes your business? Connect with us at HowToGetThereFaster.com for your free thirty-minute success call.

8

Office Hours, Couple Hours, and Do You Shut Off Work?

This question was one main reason we decided that we needed other couples to be part of this book.

We have heard of *threshold couples* who have a solid rule that once they cross certain thresholds, (the house, upstairs, the bedroom) they did not talk business.

In over three decades together, that threshold has not existed.

We *have* gotten better in some situations. When we go on vacation, we have learned how to give ourselves two time periods a day where we check email and deal with work so that we can shut it down the rest of the time. We take our anniversary off (although we launched this book on our thirtieth wedding anniversary and discussed in advance that we would be watching the best-seller numbers that day) and we take Christmas off which means that our phones are shut down. There will be other days that come up where we decide that it will be a *shut-down* day, though those days are not very common.

As we look to the future, this issue is driving how we plan our business. We are changing how we take clients (fewer) and how we structure our days to allow for more down time.

Are work hours and boundaries a challenge in your business? Let's talk about it. Connect with us at HowToGetThereFaster.com for your free thirty-minute success call.

9

When You Go on Vacation, Are You Still at Work?

"Happiness consists of living each day as if it were the first day of your honey-moon and the last day of your vacation." – Leo Tolstoy

For the longest time, it was a standing joke that if we wanted business to improve immediately, we should go on vacation. From the days before we were coaches when it was just Hank's promotional product company, we could count on always getting calls for emergency orders while we were away. Running a one-person company made that difficult.

For months ahead, we would let clients know that we would be away, and they better plan their marketing in advance.

As coaches, there are generally fewer emergencies—and we still let clients know in advance when we are going to be away.

The good thing about our business now is that we could still run our Monday mastermind call from anywhere with a high-speed internet. We would build a two-hour window into that day on the road.

We have used vacation time to finish three of our books. Twice, we have sat on the back of a cruise ship with our laptops open, enjoying the view, and another was finished while we were on vacation in Sedona before we moved to the town.

We have had to do our podcast live from the airport in Nashville because our flights were delayed twenty-four hours and we had not pre-recorded our show. We thought we would be home on time but instead, we had to do our show between gate announcements.

We often work to structure our vacation to include work time so that we can write off at least part of the trip. It might include attending a MeetUp group or getting booked for a speaking gig. Two of our best trips were serving as the continuing education for a group on a cruise ship. We enjoyed it so much that we have invited coaching clients to join us on our next cruise where we will teach or mastermind each day so that we can all write off a bit of the trip.

Are you giving yourselves enough play time? Want to talk about how to do it in your business structure? For those tips, connect with us at HowToGet-ThereFaster.com for your free thirty-minute success call.

10

Who Does What in the Business?

We have found that this is why so many people become partners in everything: They realize that together, they are more powerful.

Some partnerships come about because of a family bond (picture The Bee Gees) while others come together because they are drawn together by common interests (picture the Beatles).

In our business there are several areas where we overlap and others where we are unique.

When Hank and I tell people that we've worked together successfully for over a decade, we get odd looks as though we are unusual. It is almost as though the concept of running a business with your partner is a new thing. Sure, two unrelated people working together is common, but being together, *together* is going to put a strain somewhere.

In reality it's the way the family unit functioned for most of our development as humans and it was not until recently, the last several decades, that it has changed. Throughout history the family unit worked and played together. It was an unusual thought to leave your loved ones for any reason, let alone to work, and in any situation where productivity was essential for survival there was evidence of a family involvement. Think about working in the family store or ranch where the family is an economic, as well as social unit. It was only at the dawn of the industrial revolution that home and workplace became separate entities—each with its own set of rules.

Hank and I were not always sure that we would work together successfully, and we had contingencies in place for if we did not feel it was working for the good of our relationship. Not every challenge or large project we've taken on in our relationship has been successful. We haven't always been on the same page, but we know one thing: It is imperative to share the same passion or vision when attempting to go into business together. We have found that always maintaining focus on the bigger picture allows us to get past all the smaller issues.

There are five tips we have found to make that easier.

Define Your Roles

We each have our skills. Very broadly, Hank does most content creation and all the graphics work, while I do most of the techie stuff and handle all the human resource issues. But we each know that there is overlap and look forward to the collaboration.

Work and Play with Other People

We know that sometimes you must focus on your individuality. Though most of the time, we show up on group networking calls together, there are groups where we are the only one of our team that shows up. We each have outside interests that allow us to be in our own space.

Have a Work / Relationship Separation Policy

We can understand that the relationship comes first. Neither of us is the boss. The hard part for us, though, is to be able to turn off work. It's one of the reasons we have written this collaborative book where several couples share what works for them, and the challenges they face.

Be Honest about What You Need

The year before we got married, we saw a counsellor who helped us establish guide rules for communicating our needs. Both of us continue to work to eliminate the walking-on-egg-shells feelings that, even after thirty years together, come up. Knowing that the other is unconditionally accepted is what gets us through it. Being able to laugh at yourself helps, too.

Take Some Definite Time Away from Business

There are days that we know we take off. No client can get to us on certain holidays, especially our anniversary and our birthdays, unless we decide we will allow others to join us. When we go on vacations, the rule is that we check email in the morning and the late afternoon, and other than that, shut it off. That allows us to enjoy the rest of the time together.

The challenges we have discussed here mostly apply to couples who are romantically linked. They all can be adjusted for any two people who are in a partnership that does not involve hugs and hand holding. Remember that you began your successful business with a plan. As you've grown, your path now has many possible directions. Taking time to look at what you both want is important and should be scheduled.

Maybe one of you, or both of you, have challenges staying in the lane that best suits you. We see it all the time. If you want to talk about how it affects your business, connect with us at HowToGetThereFaster.com for your free thirty-minute success call to set up your balanced operational chart.

11

How Do You Decide on the Balance of Power?

When Sharyn joined the company, we knew that there would be a period of time when the processes that were in place would be followed.

We knew, though, that it would not take very long before Sharyn's ability to improve office systems would make that a short period.

When we moved and had to re-document the business in Arizona, we realized that it might be beneficial for this to be designated a woman-owned business, so Sharyn now legally owns 51%.

However, Sharyn's nature and background lends to her deferring to Hank more often than asserting a certain way, except in rare occasions.

But when you are on a coaching call, you definitely see that it is where Sharyn shines. She directs the calls and keeps us all on track.

Maybe one of you, or both of you, have control issues. It's common. If you want to talk about how it affects your business, connect with us at How-ToGetThereFaster.com for your free thirty-minute success call to set up your balanced organizational chart.

12

How Do You Use Your Couplehood for Marketing?

Everything in our business revolves around the fact that we are the brand. The most common version of our logo includes our both-of-us headshot. During the pandemic, we added masks to our faces on our logo.

It is rare that we appear on stage (virtually or actually) apart.

It is so rare that when one of us shows up alone at a business function, the other is immediately asked about.

This was not always the case. We had to have it pointed out to us in a very direct way.

Before we tell you this story, we should share that at the time Hank did almost every speaking engagement alone because Sharyn was not all that excited about them. It worked for us. While Hank was speaking, Sharyn could get other things done for our small business coaching clients.

Most of the time, showing up together works to our advantage and to the advantage of our clients as well as for our own marketing. We do client calls together which gives them the benefit of two marketing minds.

We also do our podcasts together. This is an example of when our marketing and deliverables are both made better by our mutual participation. After the very first episode that Hank did solo, it was very obvious that both our voices were needed if we were going to have a quality product. One voice speaking for an hour compared to two voices? Go for two. Then we added our producers into the mix and the content and flow was even better. It was also *way* more fun.

Okay, now on with the story.

We were in a coaching program with Larry Broughton—who owns a successful chain of upscale boutique hotels and who you see on the cable business channels all the time.

Larry asked us to be on his podcast. At least we *thought* he had asked us to be on his podcast. We had just started our *own* podcast and had one episode in the can, and we could promote it.

Each time Larry emailed us with details he would say something like, "Hank should be ready at 2 p.m.," and "we will need Hank's biography." We would answer each of those Hank-centric emails with answers like, "*We* will be ready at 2 p.m.," and "Here are *our* biographies."

After about four Hank-centric, us-centric back and forth emails, we decided that we should chat with Larry about this, so we called.

We explained that we were a bit confused by the emails because we were both going to be on the podcast with him. He answered very calmly.

"If you are both going to be on the show, why is Hank the only real face of your company?"

That, my friends, is a business coach getting his point across in a quite simple, direct way.

From that moment forward, we both show up for ninety-five out of every one hundred events together.

Lesson given. Lesson learned. Lesson implemented. And lesson incorporated into our own coaching programs.

Would you like to learn how to use your *couplehood* to more easily build your business and make your marketing easier? If you want to talk about how it affects your business and can be a huge benefit to your bottom line, connect with us at HowToGetThereFaster.com for your free thirty-minute success call.

13

What Is Your Hoped-For End Game?

This is an evolving discussion.

Our coaching business evolved, as planned, from the promotional product business. That business was always going to be more than just a place to get merchandise with a logo.

As we talked about in past chapters, things really changed when Sharyn joined the company. The business became something quite different and more powerful for our clients because of the skills we could bring to the table.

Had the company remained as a promotional product seller, the end game would have been to sell the client list, because that is really the best asset of those companies.

As the coaching business became more important, the end game has changed. The platform we have created could be sold to another coaching team as is but we would be incredibly diligent in determining who bought it. Remember—we searched for years to find a coaching program that we could be a part of and in the end, had to create our own. It would have to be a special coaching team to take over our program.

It may end up that the program disappears when we decide that we're done.

Would you like to talk about your end game and what steps you can take to guarantee a happy ending? Let's remove the blinders that might be in your way. Connect with us at HowToGetThereFaster.com for your free thirty-minute success call to look at your options.

14

Do You Ever Feel You Set the Bar Too High?

Yes.

And every time we set it, we reach that goal, and set another one.

As this book was being written, we had just achieved the goal that we had set twenty years ago as the end goal that would allow us to retire.

Silly us.

What hitting that goal did was give us the security to change the direction of our business the way we had always wanted to take it. We *got* to that point by learning to set goals and hold ourselves accountable to reaching them.

We have put systems in place to reach those goals. We use two systems; one is electronic, and one is a traditional paper system complete with file folders.

What is interesting, is that along the way to success, we learned to follow two rules religiously: First is to write your goals down. We have goals for our life and goals for our business. Earlier you read that this book was a few years in the making. That was because it was not yet high enough on our business goals list. As soon as it was raised into the top three, it happened. By the way, we do not just put "complete and publish *Partners In Everything*." That goal is written as "by July 2021, we have added to our list of best-selling books by completing and publishing *Partners In Everything*." Then there is a checklist of things we needed to do to make that occur.

Getting used to setting and achieving our goals has given us a freedom to be better coaches.

As small business coaches who are used to dreaming up, writing down, and achieving our goals, we have reached the point where we can coach small business owners to follow the same process.

It has allowed us to talk to a small business owner in a thirty-minute success call and quickly diagnose the causes of their challenges and give them easily achievable goals. It's one of the most pleasurable parts of our business.

By being able to set achievable goals, it helped us decide to only focus on those clients who bring us joy; those clients who appreciate they may get two points of view on a topic; clients who appreciate being able to ask any business-related question because between the two of us, we've probably encountered the issue they are being challenged with.

Goal setting is a unique challenge for couple-owned businesses. Each of you bring your personal experiences into the discussion. We goal-set on a constant basis with every one of our coaching clients. To have us help you, go to HowToGetThereFaster.com to reserve your free thirty-minute success call to plan the short term and a longer period.

15

Do You Have a Partnership Agreement?

Partnership agreements are for those unfortunate times when things aren't going swimmingly. We recommend working with a business law attorney to raise issues that might come up so that an agreement is in place to reference should those incidents unfortunately arise.

As a married couple, we know that there is an entirely different and more complicated level of issues that come into play.

If you are not a married couple, we strongly suggest that you plan for the end when things are going well and you can't imagine anything every possibly going wrong between you.

A business attorney client of ours gave us this example: Imagine you are in business with a partner and each of you are married. One of you passes away and the other is now in business with the spouse who they may have had very little relationship with previously. A great attorney will be able to walk you through this.

Would you like to look at how you are operating? Connect with us at HowToGetThereFaster.com to look at your individual situation and how to make it happen for your business.

16

Was There a Business Event That Truly Got You Focused?

Having worked with hundreds of brand-new small business owners just like you, we know the most exciting *and* the most frightening question you will have to ask yourself before starting your business will come after you do an extensive search for competition and find that there is no one in your area.

You ask, "Why isn't anyone doing this?"

Often, after a bit more research we have been able to answer that question with, "Oh, *that's* why."

In fact, we had it happen to ourselves.

We thought about opening a publishing house that would only serve brand-new business book writers. These writers would become part of the team. That team would do speaking events and workshops around the country and those workshops would leverage their expertise into business. The sales funnel was easy to sketch out. We thought it would be easy to implement our plan.

Then, we sought assistance from our advisors and after they all signed non-disclosure agreements* they asked us these questions:

- Have you ever worked with first time authors? (Yes, as a matter of fact.)

---

* When you have an idea that you are going to seek guidance to make a reality, a Non-Disclosure Agreement is necessary to protect you and your ideas from being put into action by someone else. It is not unusual for us to sign an NDA. In fact, quite often we ask for an NDA before we hear about someone's idea. They work both ways. Please do not be shy to ask someone to sign your NDA—it shows a level of professionalism and could save you a lot of money and time in court.

- If so, how many? (Well . . . one.)
- Are you ready to hand-hold them? How did it work out that first time? (Not very well.)
- How much are you going to charge them for editing? (Probably more than my editor charges me since they're new.)
- How are you going to handle publishing rights? (They will keep them.)
- How are you going to handle *all* the financial issues? (Monthly payouts?)
- How are you going to handle re-orders on the distribution platform? (Once a month order time.)
- How long will your contract be with these authors? (A year, with automatic renewals?)
- What if you don't like working with some of them? Do you have an out in your contract? (Well, we do *now*!)
- Can they publish them outside your publishing house? (Of course, but they will no longer be part of our seminar team.)
- Since all the names of the books are going to be similar (Did I tell you? It was a series and they all started with the same three words.), what happens if an author removes their title from the series? Can they re-title it?
- What if, during the writing and editing process, the author becomes too difficult to work with? (As Sharyn says, slow to hire, quick to fire.)

That kept going for about forty more what-if and are-you-kidding questions.

And yes, it could have been easy, but after we went through a series of questions, we found it was going to be expensive, too. Cost won out over effectiveness.

It should be obvious by now that we decided that our Naked Book Publishing company was going to be reserved for our books only.

This exercise of starting a new business, even though it was a division within our current business and would support our core private small business coaching business, reminded us that you should always check with those who have gone before you prior to taking that costly leap. It is what we have taught all our small business private coaching clients when they have a really cool idea and ask, "What do you guys think?"

In fact, if we don't have experience with what a client needs, we go out and get that information instead of guessing. Guessing can be costly in both time and money. So are hunches. And your gut.

It isn't that there aren't tons of incredible ideas to be thought. But we want to avoid becoming part of that statistic. You know the one. That an extremely high percentage of small businesses do not make it past the first couple of years.

Let me give you another personal story that led us to go through the exercise I just described to you.

What Adam Ace Did for Us to Solve This Challenge

We used to be part of a mastermind group that met twice a year. It was all business owners and several of us were asked to teach different sections of the breakouts. During one breakout where we were not teaching, I saw that Adam Ace was teaching and I was excited to go see what he had to share. Adam is by trade a comedian (three-time college comedian of the year) but has a good head for business.

When I walked into his session, I was amazed to be the only one in the room. Clearly, everyone figured incorrectly that Adam was *just* a comic. When he saw me, he said, "I am glad you came in . . . I have been watching what you and Sharyn are doing and I cannot figure out your focus. Lay it out for me."

At the time, we *were* lacking focus. We were business coaches first, but also had a promotional product company, offered a really cool appreciation tool through www.CardsByHank.com, and had the idea that we were going to turn that publishing company we created for our own books (Naked Book Publishing—*business stripped to the basics*) into a place where business book writers had a place to promote and sell their books. That would lead to speaking opportunities for all of us as we would create small business seminars around the country. There were also a couple of online product ideas. And . . .

Yeah . . . it was a lot.

Even as I was sketching it all out, I could see that all these projects were keeping us from focusing completely on the success we wanted to achieve for our business and our small business-owning clients.

It took twenty minutes, and I laid it all out for Adam. It was quite the flow chart. He patiently listened to all of it, then he paused and shared some words of wisdom that resonate with me years later. I share them with you now in case you are challenged with the same affliction as an entrepreneur.

"Hank," he said, "I appreciate that you are an entrepreneur. I applaud it. Truly. But . . . just because you think something would make a good business, does not mean you have to be the one to create it."

Ouch. Double ouch.

And I am going to pause here just in case you had a come-to-your-creator moment as I did.

But Adam was right. It was time to put almost everything on the back burner, or back in the freezer. Especially Naked Book Publishing. The concept of putting on seminars with lots of business experts seemed like a lot of fun, but it was not going to help us achieve our goals. It was mostly going to help them reach *their* goals without an appropriate amount of profit for the work we were going to have to put in. In fact, as we looked at it, the choice was the publishing company or our private small-business coaching practice. We had reached an important moment to make a decision.

The compromise was that we only help our coaching clients with their books and guide them through their own publishing journey.

We still offer promotional products, but they are not what we highlight in a networking situation. We still offer the appreciation tool, but mostly for the use of our clients. Well, and you, of course if you click that link.

The moral of the story is that now, each time one of us . . . okay . . . *me . . .* comes up with an idea or hears something and says, "That would be a great business idea," Sharyn smiles, looks at me and says, *"just because."*

That gets us instantly focused, I hope it does the same for you.

Do you have an idea that is burning a hole in your brain? Are you trying to figure out what could go right and what could go wrong? Let's talk about them all. Go to HowToGetThereFaster.com and register for your free thirty-minute success call. Let us be your second set of eyes.

17

Thoughts on Changing Direction and Playing to Strengths

When we moved our life and business to Sedona, Arizona in October of 2015, we changed the name of our company to Sedona Marketing Retreats because that was what we were going to do: hold marketing retreats for similar business types in Sedona. We would invite a different demographic each month (woman-owned, former military, professional, service, new business, etc.) for a three-day bootcamp designed for them. In 2017, we had been in Sedona for fifteen months and we noticed that the process was not working as well as we wanted. We decided to take our bootcamps on the road and changed our funnel to include speaking events, mostly in the three cities where we held bootcamps. We then ran the bootcamps two times a year in each city instead of one a month in Sedona.

We did this because we found out that business owners did not necessarily want to travel to Sedona if they had not yet seen us speak in person. This was backed up by our Google analytics. We found that most people were searching for us, the Yuloff name, instead of Sedona Marketing Retreats, Sedona Marketing, or marketing in Sedona. In other words, we were the draw, not our beautiful location.

Once again, it was time to play to our partnership's strengths.

To know our strengths, we must recognize a couple of our weaknesses. The most striking is a desire *to get it done now* which makes us want to over teach and makes us impatient with ourselves.

We use a number of strengths to overcome those weaknesses. Sharyn has a great ove of online tools and experimenting with them to find the very best ones.

We are also blessed with two minds that are content machines. We use and teach our clients how to use tools to get that content produced and, more importantly, repurposed so that the creation time is most valuable.

The use of those tools also gives us a head start with follow up. This gives us an equation to share with you:

The right tools + content creation + consistent follow-up = sales.

This brings us to the point of this chapter. Here are some of the lessons we learned and were taught by a once-in-a-century pandemic. More importantly, we want to answer the question, "How will we use them to make our partnership better?"

We All Need a Rainy-Day Fund

According to the Federal Reserve Bank, 40% of households didn't have enough cash on hand to cover an unexpected $400 expense. And that was before the pandemic/recession. Start to create your own safety net, even if it you are adding to it slowly. Talk to your financial advisor about a safe, liquid place to put it. If you don't have an advisor, find one by asking people you trust and interview three of them. As married partners, it can be in one fund and is part of your long-term plan as a couple. As unmarried partners, the fund must be split to take each of your family obligations in mind. How you invest that fund will probably be different.

Technology Really IS Our Friend

The adoption of online communication tools is what kept many businesses afloat. It was not a new process. The pandemic sped up the process that had already started. It amazed us how fast some business organizations that rely on membership dollars wanted to go back to IRL (in real life) experiences and the transportation time challenges that go with them. Long term, we will see how this plays out, but at this writing, we think that a hybrid model will emerge. Why would our business in Arizona refrain from sponsoring an event in Texas just because we could not show up in person? With proper pricing models, most non-profit business groups can thrive.

We had conversations with one set of partners that worked remotely. Prior to the pandemic they had been in the same office. Now, they left a Skype window open in the corner of their screen, but with the camera turned away. When they were in their office together, they would instant message the other if they needed the other one. They only turned the camera on when they were talking. This helped them continue to feel connected.

Anywhere Is Your Workplace

We knew from the beginning of our business that working from home had a lot of benefits. One of them was that when we are on the road, we always had the basics of our office with us. We placed promotional product orders from (among other places) a cruise ship docked in Sitka, Alaska and from a hotel in Florence, Italy. It was not easy, but it got done. We see a lot of large companies announcing that a work/home balance is going to become their model. Our small business coaching program has grown with red-rock views and a phone. Now that we've added visual tech, that growth is even faster.

Your team can be just as productive at home, and happier because of the flexibility it offers. It can also reduce lease expenses.

We read in a *Forbes* article that "In fact, one study by Stanford found that working from home increased productivity by 13%. The study was conducted of 16,000 workers over nine months. This increase in performance was due to more calls per minute attributed to a quieter, more convenient working environment and working more minutes per shift because of fewer breaks and sick days. Employees working from home reported that they are less distracted by co-workers, spend thirty minutes less talking about non-work topics, and spend 7% less time talking to management. Not to mention that remote work will allow much more flexibility in hiring in the future, as geographical location won't be a barrier to which jobs people can apply for, giving companies a widened talent pool."

Crowds Can Carefully Congregate

When it came to people meeting in real life, there wasn't a starter's pistol going off, it was a slow gradual coming together. As people got vaccinated and a mask became the secondary form of protection instead of primary, businesspeople cautiously eased back into normal activities. But like that nagging injury that we always pay attention to—will we always keep a wary eye open for is it back? This would be a great time for all of us to adopt a tradition I first witnessed in person in Japan. If you are not feeling well, if you just have a bit of a cold, put on a mask when you leave the house. (Because let's face it, a pandemic is not the only infectious illness that can take out the partnership.)

We see quite a few partners switching off as to who goes out to events. And others have decided that just one of them will go. For us, it is difficult since our marketing is all about us both showing up. It means that we are a bit careful as to where we go.

In-the-Office Wellbeing

We think that businesses will encourage their employees to take mental health days and to use their sick days when they are not feeling well. There will be a heightened sense of mutual responsibility for our partners and teammates. As partners, we paid a closer attention to how the other was doing. There were some webinars where one of us did even more of the talking or took over completely.

Crisis Planning

When you've been to our Small Business Breakthrough Bootcamps and some of our webinars, you have heard us talk about having plans for several types of emergencies. Among others, these have included weather, power outages, earthquakes, and individual building shut-downs. It is important to be prepared in advance so your business can continue with the least interruption. You want to respond correctly to the challenges we face, and pre-planning allows you to do that.

The only time we were completely shut down was when the power went down in our town for several hours. Our crisis plan for that now includes projects that have nothing to do with power, like reworking our studio set up, and shooting some videos on the camera's (but not our phone) battery power.

Your Online Presence

Social media proved an important way to reach new customers and stay connected with past clients. Having your digital storefront can allow you to continue in business. Along with your crisis plans, the health of your online assets should be checked constantly and updated regularly.

Reinvention Is Good

During the pandemic/recession, we got to live up to one of the things we teach our coaching clients. If you think that you can make a positive difference in your marketing, go ahead and make the change and test your theory. We went from thinking of doing *a* webinar in 2019 to doing over *a hundred* of them in 2020. We now think it is *really* odd when we hear someone in March promoting a webinar they are going to do in May. Jeepers, get *to* it already. Why wait? If it works once, you can do it again.

Our motto for 2020 was "Get Comfortable with Being Uncomfortable." It is something that is now part of our lexicon.

♦

Now that we've shared some personal insights, history, and lessons, let's hear from some other partners on these subjects.

First, we'll hear from two sets of partners in some depth—Kati and Alex Pauls, and Star and Mark Tomlinson.

Kati and Alex Pauls
KP Design

Kati and Alex are marketing tech strategists and creatives at KP Design, a digital design agency that offers entrepreneurs a full range of custom solutions to elevate their brand so they can make more money.

For my Mom - I told you so.
For Erin - You told me so.

18

Our Business and What Sets Us Apart

Our business is KP Design, and we create elevated brands. We are marketing tech strategists and creatives, specializing in building relationships with entrepreneurs by crafting elevated brands so that they reach the right people and make more money doing what they love.

An elevated brand is a guided journey to the summit of your business, successfully leading you to your brand's vision. We begin with relationship-building, developing brand strategies, creating brand assets, building websites, strategizing search engine optimization, managing social media platforms, forming digital advertising campaigns, and anything else that a client's unique situation presents.

There are boatloads of other marketing agencies out there, all doing similar (if not exactly the same) things that we do. They all promise to be the most passionate about their work, to be timely, to be supportive throughout the process, and to get you so many leads you won't know what to do with them all. So what sets us apart? What makes us stand out from the crowd?

Obviously, our delightful humour is a key factor, followed closely by relationship-building. Relationship is the foundation on which we have built our business and is a guidepost for each new project we begin. Above all else, we value our relationship with each other, with our children, with our family and friends, and with our clients. We put our relationship everywhere in our marketing and show up in our business in all our authentic glory, from social media banter to presenting at events with honesty, hilarity, and a smattering of professionalism in presenting our expertise. Time and again we are approached by prospective clients who are drawn to our relationship, and when they realize that we value our relationship with them with the same degree of passion and dedication that we have for each other, they feel safe to trust their brand with us.

Another differentiating factor is in the way that we execute creative tasks. Since tuning into our spiritual selves through meditation, we have allowed the flow of creative energy to come more quickly and more clearly, meaning we are able to provide a solution for our clients that is more meaningful to their business. The Universal Laws have come to play a bigger role in our lives as well, and since aligning with them in a purposeful way, opportunities have presented themselves to us more frequently and on a larger scale.

We work long and hard, blending the lines of business and home life to be able to offer our clients high-quality and timely solutions that, for our client, comes in the form of a smooth, easy experience right from onboarding to project completion and beyond. That is what our brand is known for and the reason we stand out in the marketplace.

19

Our Relationship

It's not easy to describe your relationship without writing a complete three-hundred-page biography. What do we leave out? What do we include? Since we've been together for so long, it'll have to go a few years back so you can understand the journey from getting to know each other to the present where we are killing it in our business thirty years later!

Once upon a time, we were born . . . kidding.

We met at the tender age of fifteen. By the way, this age seems a lot more tender now that our daughter is turning thirteen and could potentially meet her soulmate in a few years during the awkward and full-on-teenagery year of grade ten. It's cheesy to say but gosh-darn it, it's true, it was love at first sight. Love at fifteen years old is a pure, light, and introductory sort of love in which you spend most of your time exploring each other . . . we mean friendship!

As your past gently unfolds, you recognize the commonalities and admire the differences in the experiences leading up to meeting each other. One of the primary similarities between us is that we are both first-borns, meaning we had remarkably similar mindsets already before coming together. We both felt responsible for our siblings, for keeping the peace in our households, for trying to guide our siblings to keep them from making stupid mistakes, for performing our best in school or whatever activity we were involved in, and for adequately representing our family in public.

We were both first-born Canadians, neither one of us being able to speak English until we were five years old. This meant that our parents were of the same immigrant mindset, working hard and appreciating what their parents had left behind to start a new life in Canada. Our parents wanted us to build stable lives that included job security, a pension, a mortgage, and routines that kept us living in one place.

While it took Alex a little longer to realize this within himself, Kati's mindset was already one of, "I am going to make my life exactly what I want it to be, filled with adventure and spontaneity." This rocked Alex's foundation a little and every time he would get comfortable with a new stage in the relationship, Kati came at him with an idea for adventure and something bigger and better than what we were currently experiencing.

Alright, we've dated long enough, let's just get married already and start our life together. This conversation was probably brought to Alex's attention a few years before he proposed at nineteen years old. We knew there was an expectation to how long we should date before even talking about getting engaged, and because we were trying to live within the lines as much as possible to please our families, we waited. This was an example of how Alex was the perfect balance for Kati, bringing her back down to earth from the dreamworld she spent most of her time living in. She would have married Alex at sixteen years old.

You can do better than working in a factory, take something of interest in college and get going on your career. Minutes after graduating from college, Kati found an ad in the paper for power electricians to work in the province's electrical utility, which Alex promptly applied for and was hired. Kati was always telling Alex he deserved more than what he allowed himself to dream.

After two years and five moves, I am done relocating around the province, I want to buy a house in my favorite area since it's been a life-long dream to live there. Alex put in a bid for a job in the city, we bought a wonderfully old house in a snazzy area of the city, and then Alex got the job (after we bought the house). Kati always had the vision, and it was not unusual for her to get cracking on it before all the necessary ducks were in a row. There was usually a good mix of Kati pushing Alex out of his comfort zone followed by careful and strategic planning; this was not one of those times.

Now that we have one daughter and another on the way I want to build a shiny new house in a small town for our kids to grow up in. Yup, you guessed it, another vision hastily executed. We went for a drive one day, found a beautiful little community in a small town, walked into a show home, and started the process of building a house— seriously, all in one day!

I can't stay on this hamster wheel any longer, a life of adventure is calling me and it's time to answer. This time there was a good amount of planning before we pulled the ripcord on our lives. Alex left his career, we sold our home and possessions, and backpacked Europe with our kids for three months before coming back to Canada. It took all of Alex's might to remind Kati every week that there had to be a solid plan before leaving. Even though Kati pushed back a little on the timeline, she understood that he had reached a limit of spontaneity and she respected that.

You are so unhappy at your job, we've pulled the ripcord once before, let's do it again and make you an entrepreneur. Alex left his electrical career for good this time, finally knowing that he could choose the life he wanted. His mindset was permanently changed to living a life of no limitations.

This is our relationship. We challenged the mindset of our parents and dared to think outside of the realm of stability. Our desire to live a less stable and consistent life seemed like a backwards concept to our parents and often left them with feelings of worry and deep concern.

Our relationship has us challenging each other, achieving our dreams, and then starting the climb up a new and bigger mountain together. There is no such thing as a fifty/fifty relationship and if you're waiting for the teeter totter to be completely even, you'll be waiting forever. Either you'll be waiting for your partner to contribute more, or you'll feel like you're always working to pick up the slack.

At various times throughout our relationship, one of us was carrying the other. When Kati was battling depression with her hamster-wheel life in Manitoba, Alex carried her for well over a year. When Alex could barely get out of bed to go to his job when we first moved to Alberta, Kati carried him. There was unwavering strength and support during the times we were bearing the brunt of the load, one of us was always able to see the vision of where we were trying to get to and what we were trying to accomplish.

This balancing act is also true in our business relationship. There is never a moment of fifty/fifty and we consistently support each other whichever way the teeter totter leans. We understand each other's strengths and weaknesses and intuitively know when to step up our game for the other person.

Now, having said all of that, there are times when we show up as a less-than-desired version of ourselves in the relationship. We're real people with real spats and disagreements and it's taken the almost thirty years we've been together to fight in a way that doesn't completely debilitate the other person. Kati tends to be harder on Alex, especially when it comes to the business. There have been moments where she's called him out on his squirrel-like attention span or scolded him for not completing a task as quickly as she would have liked. Kati also doesn't take criticism very well and tends to shut down immediately before she can process the information. She can whole-heartedly admit there are way less times that he treats her poorly. Her frustration with him tends to happen when she feels he gets too complacent, so she boots him out of his comfort zone, and while he doesn't always like how the message is delivered, he sits with the criticism and makes an honest decision on whether it's reasonable or senseless.

Our relationship continues to grow and evolve through each new chapter of our lives. We love and respect each other and know when to offer support, give space to, or hold on to each other for dear life.

20

Our Average Workday

Kati's Average Workday

I am a creature of habit—like hardcore, crazy, *I'll-follow-you-to-the-cliff-of-a-mountain*, habit lover. When I find something that works for me, I stick to it in a religious-like fashion. For example, when I realized that homemade granola and I were meant to be in a life-long relationship (*where were you my whole life?*), I all but skip my way to breakfast each morning! I don't know what the record is for consecutive mornings eating granola, but I'm definitely in the running.

Knowing the level of dedication that goes into my habits will help you understand my average workday and that I rarely venture too far from the lovingly-crafted boundaries of this schedule.

4:00 a.m.	Wake up (5, 4, 3, 2, 1 and jump out of bed—thanks Mel Robbins)
4:00–7:00 a.m.	Work (I don't plan, I don't journal, I just sit down and work because our children, nine and twelve, are still sleeping and the house is quiet!)
7:00–8:00 a.m.	Breakfast (yup, you guessed it, granola) and a riveting round of the board game Wingspan
8:00–9:00 a.m.	A thirty-minute walk with Alex and the dog (we have the cutest damn dog you've ever seen . . . seriously, you might die if you see him) and a thirty-minute meditation session
9:00–12:00 p.m.	Work
12:00–1:00 p.m	Lunch and another game of Wingspan
1:00–1:30 p.m.	A shorter but equally necessary walk with the dog
1:30–4:30 p.m.	Work
7:00–10:00 p.m.	Occasional work and networking events

When I do wander from this schedule, it's usually to accommodate a virtual yoga session, an impromptu coffee date with a client, or to spend extra time with the kiddos. I don't follow this schedule as much on the weekends (but let's face it, entrepreneurs tend to work weekends, too). I also (habitually) throw out this schedule on Fridays!

Friday is my absolute favorite day of the week and has been since I met Alex when I was fifteen years old. Friday is *our day* just to be together. If we don't accomplish anything else but be in each other's presence, it's still a successful day. Typically, we go to the Rocky Mountains for a hard-ass hike, both to challenge and rejuvenate ourselves. Occasionally we go out for lunch and whenever the weather permits (which isn't all that often in our cold Canadian mountain climate) we take the motorcycle out and either cruise Calgary or rip through the foothills. Friday is a day of re-energizing ourselves so that we can consistently execute our schedules and be the best at what we do.

Alex's Average Workday

My average workday begins at 5 a.m. I am the opposite of Kati and am a slow riser, often lying in bed ten to twenty minutes after she's gotten up, playing with ideas and daydreaming creatively about whatever comes to mind. I follow this with a gratitude exercise and by the time I'm done, I'm ready to make the leap out of bed, leaving behind the warmth and comfort. With coffee in hand, I journal or use the quiet time to plan the day/week and make notes of what I need to accomplish. After that I check my email and take care of any outstanding tasks from the day before.

At 7 a.m. it's time to wake up the girls, feed an extremely excited dog, and make sure Kati has enough coffee in her so she feels human enough to interact. I can't tell you how often I have walked past her desk to find her working away, her first coffee of the morning sitting half-drunk beside her. My experience tells me this is not enough for her to happily talk to other humans! Kati religiously washes the dishes (she has a minor habit problem) while I make cereal for the girls and then set up a board game for us to play while we eat, and we all spend some time together.

Before 8 a.m. we are all out the door and the kids walk three minutes to school as we walk our dog (Bear) together and discuss work, the world, our ideas, and our goals. Some days it's big picture stuff where we plan our big dreams, and other days it's the little stuff like just making it to lunchtime and accomplishing enough before the kids get home, and we are forced to stop.

Our family quality time revolves around us eating together, and we all take that time to be present for each other. There's no TV anywhere near our dining area and there are no cell phones at the table, which means work is turned off. It gives us all a chance to unplug from the outside world to focus on each other.

My afternoons (1 p.m. to 5 p.m.) consist of phone calls, Zoom calls, and meetings with a little bit of heavily interrupted task completion in between. This is my favorite part of the day as I am very social and love speaking to our clients and networking with amazing people from all over Canada and the U.S.

At 5 p.m. we all come together again, have a little bit of good quality wine while cooking (there's nothing better than an excellent bottle of wine—it's one our great joys). I will often play a game with the kids if they don't complain too loudly about it, and wrestle with the dog or attempt to play a game of fetch where the ball is never returned. Apparently, huskies just chase things down and then go bury the item like a squirrel to save it for another day.

After dinner we go for another walk together to decompress. Sometimes there is a lot to say, and sometimes there is not even one word spoken. Walking is the key to many things in our daily lives. It has always been a pillar of our success as a couple and as individuals. Once we've got the blood moving again and we walk off the meal and the wine, it's time to finish up the day with completing some final work tasks while getting set up for another day by making notes for the 5 a.m. version of future me.

Between 8 p.m. and 9 p.m. it is the final stretch of quality family time which consists of the kids and me reading together, watching something funny on TV, and helping with conveniently forgotten homework/assignments for school instead of getting ready for bed. By 10 p.m. it's bed for everyone. I'm sure the girls are reading, drawing, or playing with their toys one last time before they finally pass out which I'm totally okay with as long as they stay in their rooms.

10 p.m. for us is the last bit of decompression where we can talk, read fiction, and watch a couple of YouTube videos. We look back on a full day that started so long ago at 5 a.m. that you thought it was yesterday and are grateful for all that was accomplished, and of the people who took part and played a role in making it a unique and amazing day.

As I was writing this section, I reflected on my average corporate workday which had looked something like this: wake up at 6 a.m., shower, leave immediately for a one-hour commute, sit in a cubicle for the mandatory eight and half hours, commute one hour home, eat, play with the girls for an hour before their bedtime, then play video games to escape the thoughts of the cubicle and what was to come the next day. It's no wonder that life was completely unsustainable and soul crushing because it was the completely wrong life for me.

Now I wake up at 5 a.m., full of gratitude, then allow the ideas and the possibilities of a new day to flow in.

21

Power Couple

Kati's Definition

Upon first considering the term *power couple* I instinctively threw it out the window, associating it in my mind with masculine-like energy that sets out to conquer and obliterate anything in its path. This is definitely not Alex and me. Defining *power couple* had me puzzled and so I set out for my morning walk every morning for a week with the intention of coming up with a definition that worked for me. Funny thing about throwing a question out to the universe is, if you can get still enough and quiet enough, the answer will come. So early one morning, on the breath of the wind as I stood looking out over the Alberta foothills, I heard the universe reply.

For us, *power couple* means that each of us is deeply connected to our personal power and allow a respect for the other's natural abilities to come forward. We strive to set aside ego to allow a coming together of our creative energies.

In my mind, when you can connect to your own power, you are able to show up in the relationship as your most authentic self. It's in this purity of who you are that you are able to hold space for your partner's authentic self to join. When this happens, your gifts and talents are magnified by the power of co-creation.

This, to me, is the true meaning of a power couple. It's in this magic that we can successfully be partners in everything.

Alex's Definition

When I used to hear the term *power couple,* I often pictured two professionals like a CEO and a doctor that were very successful when it came to their careers, with a lavish lifestyle, who happened to be married. Whether or not they were happy was none of my business.

67

That was my old way of thinking. The present day me believes a real power couple use their individual strengths to help elevate their partner in weaker areas. They step up for their partner in situations or in tasks that are better suited for the other's strengths. You always have each other's backs no matter what. It's like the Godfather, you never go against the family.

The real *power* we have found comes from combining both of our similar strengths and exponentially catapulting ourselves towards our goals. It's so important to be on the same page and work towards a common goal, rather than one person dreaming of a house in the Bahamas and the other wanting a ranch in Montana to raise sheep for mutton bustin' competitions. We have often played in our imaginations together with our distant future selves. We dreamed big, or what we used to think was big and we would go for it. The best example was our dream home that we custom built at the age of thirty-two. To go from a one-bedroom apartment eating fifty-cent burritos and trying to make it through college while being crushed by student loans, and only having one pair of pants at the age of twenty-four . . . to an "impossible goal" in eight years is incredible as I look back and connect the dots of that journey in my mind.

Accomplishing goals and dreaming *big* are great, but it's all for nothing if your relationship suffers or ends. A true power couple finds ways to always take the time to strengthen their relationship because without that foundation, everything will crumble, and the journey together ends. Is money and success worth growing apart from the person that matters most to you? The real power comes from the strength of our bond, the love and respect we have for each other, and keeping our priorities in a specific order to maintain balance. We take care of ourselves and each other first and foremost. That way we can be our best selves, to be there for our children, dog, our business, and the people in our lives.

22

Our Office Space

Our office for the most part is wherever we are, and thanks to the pandemic, we have had to get creative— there were a few months when Kati was working out of the bedroom closet. We live in a very modest home which can often feel quite small. There are times Kati sets up an office in the bedroom while Alex works in the basement (when it's not being occupied by our AirBnb guests); sometimes Kati builds an office around the bed, positioning a large monitor on a stool while holding her laptop on her legs; sometimes Alex sets up at the dining room table for as long as he can stand getting up every few minutes to let the dog in and out of the house.

Before the lockdowns, we would work from our local coffee shop a few times a week just to be able to interact with the energy of other people. There are times we work from the car, just driving to the mountains and back, discussing work and our business goals. Sometimes, we work while we're hiking, waiting for inspiration from nature. One of our favorite places to work is on the motorcycle! Once the helmet goes on, our minds become still enough to create new ideas for our business without interruption (of course Kati's mind is more at liberty to wander in this way while Alex has to focus on the road).

Most of the time we each work from a small desk in the common area upstairs which works the best when our children are in school and not stopping in front of us, asking for this or that on their way from their bedrooms to the kitchen to rummage for food. One of Kati's favorite office tech pieces is her noise-cancelling headphones which creates a feeling of being alone to be able to access her creativity (also it blocks out Alex's muttering as he tends to curse at his computer when it's not behaving). We do our Zoom meetings from this common space, muting ourselves when the kids are loudly walking through with their friends. We try not to get angry with them since we're the ones who have set up an office almost directly in their hallway, two steps from their bathroom. This is a result of working primarily from home and in a house that is not large to begin with.

The upside of this arrangement is that it gives us all a sense of closeness that would not exist if we worked outside of the home or lived in a bigger house. The kids also get a first-hand view of what it takes to start a business and turn it into a success. They get to observe how a married couple can also be a working couple—we are role models for them of how a married couple should treat each other, both at home and in a business situation. When they grow up, they'll know that they deserve nothing less from their future relationships, personal or business.

The idea of an office space outside of our home is alluring some days; it's those days when we are feeling particularly annoyed with each other, or the dog, or the children, or the lack of space that we fantasize about driving to an office and closing the door to be productive for a few hours. What we have learned however, is that when we are feeling this way, it's usually time to take a break, get out into nature, exercise a bit, and then come back and try again. More often than not it works like a charm.

23

The Story of Our Business and How We Became Partners

If we're going to talk about how KP Design started, we'll have to go back to how it started for Kati more than twenty years ago. Kati was bred to become a musician from a young age and followed it through with a Bachelor of Music degree from the University of Manitoba. Ever the entrepreneur, Kati started her own studio at fourteen years old and taught flute and piano, quickly realizing her disdain for working in close proximity with children. Despite this, she was committed to establishing a successful studio, even when we had to move to the middle of nowhere in Northern Manitoba, not once, but twice for Alex's career. During one of these rotations in the great north, Kati began teaching herself how to code websites with good old-fashioned HTML and CSS. Coding provided a refreshing intellectual outpouring from the left side of Kati's brain, giving the right side a much-needed rest. When a large daycare centre in Winnipeg was looking to create a digital presence, they reached out to Kati, and she designed and developed her first website (the first of four websites she would end up doing over the next twenty years for this daycare!) and was immediately hooked.

As we continued to move around the province for Alex's training rotations every six months, Kati finally closed her music studio and focused on learning everything she could about website design and development. Most of it was self-taught through books (YouTube was not the wealth of educational videos that it is today) and the rest was filled in with a few courses from the local community college in Winnipeg. In fact, it was after completing a hefty JavaScript course at Red River College that Kati's instructor introduced her to a woman who was looking to hire a website designer for her own web design business.

Working alongside this business-minded woman would be as close to an entrepreneurial mentorship as Kati would ever receive. Learning an invaluable amount on how to run a successful web design business, KP Design was born, and Kati began a boutique graphic design and web design studio that unbeknownst to her would one day employ her husband and grow to be one of the top 10 best graphic design businesses in Calgary, Alberta.

KP Design was always more of a supplemental job that Kati did in the background of Alex's career which worked out well as we had started our family and raising the girls had become her primary focus.

Then, in 2016, after a year of personal defeat, loss and family chaos, Kati and Alex decided it was time for a major reset. We were standing at the edge of a cliff; behind us was our beautifully custom-built dream home, Alex's successful fifteen-year career (successful as in he had managed to make several moves up the corporate ladder), our happily settled children and two senior cats, and Kati's graphic design studio. However, the weight of knowing we were meant for something bigger, something newer and more adventurous had us leap off the cliff into the unknown! Alex left his career, we sold our house and most of our belongings, and with our two young children in tow (they were five and eight at that time) set off to Europe with nothing but our backpacks. We traveled to eleven different countries over the duration of three months, beginning in Ireland and ending in Hungary, at which point we felt ready to return home, although we would never again live in the province we grew up in, and our Alberta chapter began.

With a fresh mindset, Kati threw herself into KP Design and actively sought out new clients while continuing to take care of her Manitoba clients, and slowly the business began to grow.

Alex had started a new job with a mentor from his previous career. Looking back, taking the leap was terrifying, but Alex landed in familiar waters to help minimize the shock. The thought process of going into business with his mentor was to learn from a successful businessman, who ran a small business very profitably, and where every person at the company was extremely important to the operation. The long-term plan was to become part owner of the company and then usher in a new wave of energy and success once the torch had been passed.

Unfortunately for Alex, his mentor suddenly passed away nine-months after he started, and his training and mentorship was far from complete. Devastated, he found himself not in a position to move forward in the company without his mentor and turned to another opportunity that had presented itself a few months before. He turned to working remotely for a friend's company within the same industry where his skills could easily be transferred and utilized. Within a short amount of time, despite a valiant effort, the square peg and the round hole just weren't meant for each other. Again, Alex was wrecked and felt that he let his good friend down by being the wrong man for the job, and the situation left him questioning his self-worth.

In hindsight (which is always twenty/twenty), this was the greatest gift for Alex. He had finally been pushed off the correct mountain top and into his true calling. The plunge into that ice-cold glacial water awoke the person he so desperately wanted to become but didn't know how to get there.

After grieving as hard as possible for the death of the 2018–2019 version of Alex Pauls, the new Alex was born and with the unwavering support of Kati who helped him repair his damaged self-worth, he put together all the new pieces that would be needed to go along with an already strong technical and analytical skill set. Kati and Alex agreed it was finally time to join forces because there was no denying it now, it was what was meant to be all along— working together was always the dream!

Alex on Joining His Wife's Already Established Business

Being an already established business and not knowing exactly how protective of her company's integrity Kati was, she sat me down to clarify explicitly how important integrity was to her company and that there was very little room for my squirreliness. "We do what we say and we do it quickly and well! We don't stop until the task is done!" Wow! This was a wakeup call for me. My respect grew for her tenfold as I felt the pride and love that she had put into this business, and I quickly adopted that same love as if it were another child. It didn't take long for KP Design to become *ours*, as I worked as hard as possible to get up to speed. Meanwhile, I consistently showed up for her and presented her business in a way she never could express herself because of her extremely humble nature.

I am not humble when it comes to my amazing wife! She walks into a room and her energy lifts me up every time. When I talk about her and the things she creates for people, it is honestly the easiest thing I have ever had to say to anyone. I don't even consider it selling, which is probably why I am so good at it. There is absolutely no pressure for me to speak openly and honestly about the gifts that she has, and how valuable she is to everyone we work with.

That first conversation really set the stage for me. It forced me to get over myself, to face any ego issues I had about working for, and with, my wife, and flush that mindset immediately, which was the key! It's not about me, it's about us, and the journey we are on together in growing this business.

In the fall of 2019, Alex started working at KP Design as the business development and SEO specialist. For the rest of the year, we focused on networking, meeting as many entrepreneurs as we could at a multitude of events. It was incredible how quickly we signed on clients looking for digital marketing solutions after only spending a few minutes interacting with them. We realized that's where the magic was, our secret sauce if you will, and we put our relationship out there front and center and connected with entrepreneurs as a couple in business. Even as we grow and take on more employees, our relationship remains the flagship of KP Design.

24

Office Hours versus Couple Hours

Kati

I have an extremely hard time flipping the closed sign on our business and tend to stay open almost 24/7. Some of it has to do with my personality and how I'm built, but the other part is since this business is something that I have grown out of nothing. Failure is not an option, and while we're figuring out our growing pains, my brain wants to run full speed ahead to make sure we're delivering the best to our clients in a reasonable amount of time.

I am grateful daily that Alex has come on board in this business, for so many reasons, but mostly because he saves me from myself constantly. When I ignore my body's cries for help, he hears them loud and clear and forces me to stop and focus on something else. He makes sure that I take time to play a game, get outside, or work on a puzzle. Even my twelve-year-old daughter walks past me, sees my bulging veins, and quickly brings me a glass of water to hydrate.

I am aware of how lucky I am to be uplifted and cared for by the people closest to me in my life; it's a colossal contributing factor to my success. I am also learning to reprogram my brain to recognize when I am no longer being productive or when I need to spend time on self-love. I don't know if it's a male thing or if it's specific to Alex, but I envy the way he can turn off work when he doesn't feel like doing it. He might just outlive me if I don't shift my mindset and start taking better care of myself.

When I am able to switch from work hours to couple hours, I sure am grateful I did and love every minute (except when he's being an ass during my "ladies' days"). We tend to know and sense when it's the right or wrong time to discuss business, which after a few heated arguments, becomes easier to discern. It's important to allow the heated moments to happen so they can shape the way you want to interact with each other. The mastery of conflict resolution is one of the keys to a successful relationship for both office hours and couple hours. It's important to understand that arguing is okay, and that it's the quality of the resolution that will determine whether it was worth arguing about in the first place.

Here's how the typical argument goes for us (keep in mind we're not talking about actually physically hurting each other, this is a battle of words).

One of us pisses the other off, usually by way of escalated mental poking, to a point where we decide *not to let this one go*. Alright, the gloves are off and we're in fight position, ready to defend our opinion to the bitter end. We throw a punch, blocked. We throw another punch, blocked. So far so good, somewhat civilized, not too much blood, let's keep going. Jab, jab, jab.

This is where years of experience and the wisdom of maturity shows up to keep one of us from throwing a knockout blow. We've each said what we need to say in order to secure our position in this fight and it's time to take a step back. We know our roles. Kati is a Scorpio, which means she's stubborn as hell and is most likely to defend her position to the grave. Alex is a Virgo and would rather not engage in conflict in the first place and is almost always the one to soften the tension by putting out fire with a soothing phrase, something like "this has gotten out of hand, let's go for a walk."

Going for a walk is the perfect distraction for me to quickly remove myself from the blazing fire I've created. Then during the walk, the argument turns into a discussion, and when we're not having to face each other but instead focused on the ground in front of us, somehow it disarms us and allows reasonable back-and-forth to occur. This is our conflict-resolution process and what works for us. If there's no time for a walk, we shelve it and save it for a time when we can get out into nature. Figure out how to recognize when the argument has escalated to its boiling point, learn what technique will work to turn down the heat a little, and then work through the rest of the argument in a non-confrontational way so neither of you gets burned.

Alex

Our life and our business are completely intertwined in a very harmonious way. We each experience different stresses when it comes to our business at different levels, intensities, times. We have had the luxury of one of us breaking down at a time, so the other was there to pick up the pieces and help in the best way possible to support the other.

We began working out religiously together three years ago at Orangetheory Fitness (shoutout and high praises to the OTF family!) way before we were business partners. We quickly realized the significance our physical health was to our overall health (mental/physical/spiritual). Our confidence and fitness levels were incredible and at forty I was in the best shape of my entire life! It's impossible to be your best self when your health is not in balance. There's a reason people are posting selfies of themselves working out in the gym. It's not with the intention to shame the rest of us for laying on the couch participating in a six- hour Netflix binge. It's to celebrate how good they feel, and that they accomplished something truly challenging. "Tough times don't last, tough people do" repeats over and over in my head every time I want to give up on anything that is challenging.

I am fortunate that I can shut off work very easily and focus on the children or do projects around the house which I enjoy doing. At this point with KP Design, Kati needs me to take a good chunk of the daily parenting role while she is creating. We are both raising our daughters to be independent on a daily basis. We fell in love with the quote from Michelle Obama's mom, "I'm not raising children, I'm raising adults." I am asking more and more of them as I show them that we are a family unit, and we take care of each other, the house, and the dog together. Mom might be a religious dish washer, but they know that Dad will help by loading or unloading the dishwasher. It has taken longer than I would like to admit, but we will make sure they will be ready for the real world when it comes time to move out of the nest.

All that being said, when I am in the zone and I am focused intensely on something, it is like waking a grizzly bear from hibernation if someone disturbs me. It takes a lot of effort for me to calm my squirrely brain down and enter *the zone*. So, when I'm there, it's wise not to poke the bear. It is the only time when I am very serious, and I turn into a completely different version of myself. I probably wouldn't even recognize myself if someone sent me a video of me in *the zone*."

There might come a time in the future when things change and I go through a period where it is impossible to shut off work, even while I sleep. This was definitely the case for me a few years ago as my Friday nights and Saturdays were my only reprieve from the coming week. By Sunday morning I was already dreading what was to come and preparing the necessary chess moves to try and navigate the minefield and hopefully make a sale.

For now, I will be grateful that I can take the time to recharge and come back to my desk and be the best version of myself because of the ability to completely focus on the present moment with my loved ones.

Our couples' hours are all throughout the day. I am definitely the more affectionate one, I will kiss or hug Kati randomly when my squirrleyness takes over and I must move around the house. I send love notes via text message which I'm sure are totally distracting and I get offended when I'm ignored. I love to get Kati coffee in the morning and make sure the thermostat is set high enough so that I don't have to hear about how cold the house is, while simultaneously showing her how much I care.

The multiple walks we take throughout the day are filled with both personal and work-related topics as we hash out the challenges we are facing or polishing some really good rough ideas we had from a previous walk or brainstorming session. When we need to shut off a couple of times a day, we set up a board game for ourselves and just focus on having some fun while engaging our brains in something creative other than work.

25

Working While on Vacation

Here's the scoop, a few months after Alex joined KP Design, a little something called the pandemic hit, and all travel plans were cancelled. In fact, we were set to take a three-week vacation driving along the coast to California when they closed the international borders one day before we were meant to leave.

Fortunately, we were able to take a few mini trips during the pandemic and explored a few of our own provinces in Canada, stopping in the Okanagan Valley (a few too many times perhaps) to pick up the best wine around! Because our business had doubled during the pandemic year, we had to keep working while we were away on these mini trips.

So, the work came with us. That's the beauty of being an entrepreneur, especially when you can work from any location like we can. As long as there's an internet connection, we're ok to work from a hammock in our bathing suits. However, even though we're on vacation, there still must be some form of structure for getting work done. Now that you've read the section on our typical workday, we'll paint the picture of our typical vacation workday.

Being on vacation for us doesn't mean sleeping in. In fact, the time between 4:00 a.m. and 10:00 a.m. becomes the most valuable time to get work done. It's during this time that the other people in our party (kids, parents, friends) are taking advantage of sleeping in and resting their bodies for another day of fun. For us, it's six hours of productivity being propelled by the vision of us walking away from our computers to partake in the fun with everyone else. Nothing makes us work more efficiently than when we set a goal and a reward for completing that goal. Then after everyone has settled in for the evening, we set up for a few more hours of work if necessary.

Even though Kati is committed to her typical workday schedule, and even though she has a hard time turning work off in her mind, something about being on vacation allows her to do so guilt-free! This makes vacationing even more worthwhile! It's not just the destination, but the adapted mindset to allow for more downtime and fun that becomes the true benefit of travel. So much of our creativity comes from our vacations as we allow for the recharging of our batteries.

One of the biggest adjustments Alex had to make was shifting his mindset from punching in and punching out at set times of the day to working when it felt right to work. However, along with this kind of freedom comes the responsibility to work even when we're on vacation.

It is an awesome feeling to be able to take care of our business and all of the relationships we have created without skipping a beat. If we are in Disney World on a Monday, that's what our out-of-office reply is set to. By Tuesday morning (3:00 a.m. to 4:00 a.m.) all fires have been put out or at least dealt with accordingly. We would highly recommend this type of arrangement for everyone that owns their own business. The amount that you will be able to accomplish once you leap out of bed and the caffeine starts flowing, you will wonder why you have never tried this before! If you need a nap by the pool in the afternoon, no one will judge you. You're on vacation!

26

Who Does What in the Business

We think it's important to break this down into sections: what our roles are in the business as well as what we think the *other* person's role is. Having a solid understanding of what you do in the business and what your partner does is one of the key elements in making your business and personal relationship copasetic.

Kati: What I Do In The Business
I am a marketing tech strategist and the creative director at KP Design; I also hold the vision for our business.

As a marketing tech strategist, my job is to connect with a client, figure out where they are on their branding journey, strategize a plan, and then build a custom solution for them. My role includes offering my expertise and then guiding the client through the processes with relative ease and unbridled joy. Let's face it, there's nothing better than having an expert take on something that has had you stumped in your business for a long time! This role has allowed me to get clear on the client journey and create processes to facilitate a seamless set of branding steps.

As the creative director I am responsible for all graphic design tasks from designing websites, to creating brand assets, to curating social media posts. Of course, this includes a large list of other graphic design services, all of which I am solely responsible for executing. This role takes many, many hours of my time because it not only includes producing the tangible elements required but requires the time it takes to tap into my creative energy. Granted the time it takes to get into the creative groove has become significantly less since I started meditating, something I should have done right from the beginning. It's remarkable how quickly I can get a download of inspiration for creative work when I'm centered, still, and in the mode of receptivity. Perhaps this is one of the biggest misunderstandings about graphic designers; we do not sit at our computers moving clipart around or haul out our easels and paint in wheat fields. We ground, center, and allow creativity to flow through us, bringing clarity on how to reflect a visual solution to a problem. In its simplest form, we are creative problem solvers.

My superpower is holding the vision for our business. This requires a deep understanding of our goals and the capacity to hold space for the vision to come about, however it's going to happen. Sometimes I get caught up in *how* we will make it happen before I remember to step back and *allow* it to happen. As the keeper of the vision, all business decisions come back to me so I can gauge how it resonates with our long-term objectives. In this way, I am in a CEO position within our company. This is yet another term which doesn't sit well in my mind, so I never use it to describe my position . . . vision keeper is so much better!

Kati: What I Think Alex Does in the Business

Alex is also a marketing tech strategist and creates strategies for our clients from a slightly different perspective than me. He views our client's business from an end-game angle, meaning he strategizes the short and long-term goals for getting in front of the right people, and selling the right products and services to them. I often work the most on the first half of the client journey, setting up the brand strategy, designing the assets, and building the website before I hand off the baton to Alex to take them the rest of the way. He steps in with his SEO expertise, optimizing the copy as well as the images on the website, and then designs the marketing campaigns using Google Ads and social media ads. It has become a beautiful workflow of each of our strengths filling in the gaps to create a seamless client journey.

Alex oversees business development. He keeps an eye out for opportunities to get in front of entrepreneurs who could benefit from our services. When someone reaches out to us, Alex connects with them right away to set up a conversation. He is incredibly good at interacting with other humans and is often the reason our clients end up being our friends. He has a deep understanding of the value of listening and allowing the client to talk about themselves and their problems. He naturally makes those around him feel at ease by showing up authentically in each interaction. Yes, there are times when his humor is off-putting to those not in touch with their inner stand-up comedian, but it doesn't happen often.

Alex also has another vital role in our business and one that I've touched on in an earlier section—to save me from myself! I don't mean that in a damsel-in-distress-way, but rather in the way he helps me be the best version of myself. These tasks include:

- Calling me out when I'm playing too small
- Forcing me to stop working when I'm not being productive
- Being the more-present parent for our kids when I'm in the middle of a project
- Picking up dog poo when I'm too tired to bend over and do it myself
- Reminding me of our vision when I get caught up in how I can make it happen

Alex: What I Do in the Business

My role at KP Design has quickly evolved from business development specialist and SEO expert to co-owner of a marketing tech strategy company that focuses on taking our clients' businesses to the next level and beyond. It won't be long before I am delegating the tasks that I created for myself to our trusted employees, in order to focus on growing our business to a top-five agency in Western Canada.

I love project management and creating ad campaigns that net great results! I enjoy playing with the Rubik's cube in my head while I craft the perfect ad copy and target audiences. I have always found complex games to be the most fun. Don't get me wrong, I will play Pie Face with my kids just to make them laugh, but I get real joy out of creating a booming business settlement while playing Terraforming Mars against my friends.

A huge part of what I do at KP Design are the website audits, the SEO maintenance and setup, and meeting with people every day to discuss how we can help each other or if we know anyone who could help the other with a specific need. I also enjoy creating content for ourselves via the KP Design blog, books, and our eventual podcast.

Some additional roles I have naturally taken on include professional hype man for the world's most talented graphic design artisan/super mom, as well as professional driver/motorcycle tour guide extraordinaire.

Alex: What I Think Kati Does in the Business

Kati is the most disciplined person I have ever met. She honestly is not happy relaxing. I can't remember the last time she sat and watched a movie. "It's a complete unproductive waste of time," I am told. She will however work on the couch occasionally when the kids and I watch *The Office* together.

She is constantly doing something for our business, I feel bad going to the washroom sometimes because I am trying to keep up with her sitting-in-front-of-the-computer stamina. Meanwhile, I'm watching crows fight over a piece of garbage in the street. I'm laughing and pointing like a first grader while she reaches for her noise cancelling headphones and nonchalantly tunes me out.

Kati creates beautiful designs every single day, which is incredible to me. I will give myself credit though, I don't love all the things she creates which makes for an interesting exchange because I always let her know if I don't care for a design and then we go over the details. If you're going to criticize a pro you better have something constructive to back it up!

One of my favorite parts of working together is networking as a team. I am so confident when I am with her. Her loyalty is her greatest strength, and it does not matter what I say or do, she will always back me up. The thing that surprised me the most when we started working together was how good she is at expressing herself in public situations and in presentations, relaying information to people, and how organized she is. I knew she was those things, but it's a totally different experience when you get to be their shadow and watch how they operate. I catch myself looking at her and just saying "wow" in my head every time.

Kati is an incredible writer and editor for our blogs, website, and social media content. But most importantly, she is the dreamer of our tag-team. She is already crafting ideas and goals as I sit down on top of the figurative mountain we just climbed trying to take in the view. She is the opposite of complacent. When I hear one of her wild ideas that resonates with me, I let her know that I am totally on board. This is after years of me resisting. I know better now, because she knows the only way to get where we want to be is to dream it.

27

The Balance of Power

We think it's important to define what *balance of power* means. For us, it's the sweet spot in which we are performing work functions at our best within a collaborative framework. Again, it's not a matter of things being fifty/fifty, but rather having a clear set of responsibilities and roles that play to the person's strengths and abilities. Whatever the percentage of work being divided comes to, is neither here nor there. We have no idea what percentage of work each of us has in the business, only that when a project starts, we each bring our skills to the table to offer the best possible solution for the client.

Within this balance of power there are micro scenarios where things are more noticeably unbalanced.

For instance, money and financial decisions. We don't always agree on what we should spend the money on within the company. If it were up to Alex, we would always have money in savings just in case shit hits the fan, and another chunk of money in investments, growing over time. While he's not wrong, Kati has other ideas for the money which include traveling, buying nicer office furniture, and splurging more often on expensive bottles of wine. Because Alex has a knack for numbers and his feet planted a little more firmly on planet Earth, he makes most of the financial decisions.

When it comes to making big picture decisions for the company, Kati tends to have final say as the vision keeper for the business. If the roles were reversed Alex would have KP Design pumping out everything from Shopify sites to hiring magicians who pose as graphic designers when they're not making psychedelic YouTube videos of themselves flying through the air (this might be a reference to an actual situation last year).

What Happens When One of Us Doesn't See the Lack of Balance within the Company?

We are not a fairy tale 100% of the time—close, but not all the time. Pointing out your partner's blind spots within the business is as tricky as casually mentioning they've gained a few pounds. So how do we tackle this?

We have a high-performance coach that we defer to in these situations. Her telling Kati that she needs to get over herself and hire a graphic designer to do the same kind of work she's capable of producing goes over a lot better than Alex telling her the same thing (although Kati did hit the mute button on that particular zoom call and did an amazing impersonation of a ventriloquist spewing out obscenities without so much as separating her lips).

Our high-performance coach telling Alex to man-up and do a task he's been avoiding isn't interpreted as instructions coming from a nagging wench, but as our coach pushing Alex to be better and get the job done.

It's invaluable to have a business coach for so many reasons, but for this reason it's worth it. Having a third party to help us push through our own mental glass ceiling forces us to grow in uncomfortable, but necessary ways.

28

Using Couplehood for Marketing

We know that the secret sauce to our business is our couplehood and we make sure our relationship is front and center in all of our marketing. It allows a certain degree of relatability with our clients and also expands our target audience to include both men and women.

If you look at our website, the first visual elements you'll see are photos of us together, both in a business and personal setting. There is no question that our business is a collaboration of our unique strengths.

Our Instagram and Facebook profiles are photos of us not just working together but actually living life with kids and a dog. Spending time on our social feeds allows you a sneak peek into our day-to-day happenings. The posts featuring us are real, not posed, and typically on the funnier side. It's especially important on social media to be relatable, authentic, and human.

When Alex is a guest on podcasts (something he's been doing a lot lately) he always mentions the importance of our relationship and often shares humorous anecdotes of things that have happened to us. Besides the obvious entertainment value, this makes us more relatable and down to earth, hopefully already building a sense of relationship with our potential clients.

Our branding voice is light, engaging, and authentic; we don't bullshit people with fancy words and promises of immediate riches for hiring us over one of our competitors. There is always a sense of being in the middle of a good conversation with a friend in our copy, whether it's in our blogs or on our social media platforms.

We always show up together for networking events and other business engagements. When people think of KP Design, they think Kati *and* Alex; neither one of us has a more important role than the other in the mind of our client.

29

The End Game and How We Will Leave

As often happens in relationships, we initially had two different scenarios in mind for the end game. We're not talking about our life's end game (Alex has that all planned out including a DeLorean and the Grand Canyon for our eightieth birthdays). We're talking about our goal for KP Design and how we will leave the business.

Alex's vision: *For the girls to take over the business and make it their own.*

Kati's vision: *To sell for several million dollars and start another business.*

When we combined our answers together, we were essentially saying the same thing. Wherever we are at, whether it's KP Design or another company that we've grown, our hope is that our kids have the entrepreneurial bug and will want to join or take over our business.

I guess you could say our hoped-for end game is that we've positively influenced our children to dare to dream, show up big in the world, and make their lives exactly what they want it to be. If we are talking about goals specific to the business, it would be to grow the business to be worth $5,000,000, sell it, and use the money to start another business (more than likely a bed and breakfast with services such as healing sessions, nature hikes, and yoga). KP Design has been an incredible experience of learning the ins and outs of growing a business, and everything we've learned could be applied to another business venture in the future. We are in the business of building relationships with people and providing a high-quality service to help others grow. This can also be achieved in the hospitality/wellness industry and hopefully allow for a slightly slower pace.

When I look back on our years running KP Design, I will remember the hard work and long hours of maintaining the high standards we set for ourselves. While I genuinely love a good challenge, there are many times I crawl to the bedroom and fall into bed, eyes screaming tired, and completely exhausted from consecutive hours of creative work.

When the time comes to leave the business, Kati will be skipping in a meadow of flowers towards her yoga hut on her acreage, sitting in stillness and enjoying every second of peace, occasionally baking bread and making granola. You will find Alex happily driving a van full of wine enthusiasts between our bed and breakfast and the finest vineyards in the Okanagan, regaling them with tales of the migratory patterns of unique birds to motor-cycle adventures in Central America.

We're sure KP Design will not be our last collaborative venture since it's been fun (a lot of work, but fun) learning new things, growing together, and helping other entrepreneurs be successful in their businesses.

30

Measuring Success

When it comes to measuring success, do you ever feel you've set the bar too high?

Kati: YES!
I am often a victim of setting the bar too high for myself. When I set impossible goals, and then don't achieve them, I spiral in the depths of despair. The crazy thing is that I keep doing it to myself, knowing full well a meltdown is imminent, and then during the meltdown giving myself the same pep talk, "you know you're going to do it anyway, just suck it up and get off the floor and back to work."

There is a lesson in setting the bar too high for myself and I keep repeating it because I haven't caught on, but I'm working on it. I also set the bar too high for those around me, setting them up for failure as well. It's so easy to aim for the stars and demand excellence all the time when you've built a business from the ground up with your sweat and tears. There is a lesson in setting appropriate goals for yourself and your business partner which are quickly coming to light for me.

Because of my crazy high-bar setting, it also means I often don't see the success and am therefore not measuring it accurately. I've had Alex look up from the computer and air high-five me for a social media graphic I created for a client. "Dude, this graphic is killer." And I stop, look, and think, "Huh, it is a killer graphic, isn't it?" I perhaps hadn't heard back from the client about its awesomeness and assumed it didn't go over well enough to deserve a mention or a thank you so I wrote it off as mediocre work.

Even within a successful business there is room to grow and be better, that's why coaches exist! There are times when I think that even she sets the bar too high for me. "Crazy lady doesn't know what she's asking of me, it's not like she has to do it," is not an uncommon reaction for me. But I always come around and realize that I am able to reach a little higher than I thought I could, and what's funny is I probably would have set the bar higher than that for myself in the first place but wouldn't have succeeded. Coaches are smart and I respect the hell out of mine! *(Mental note for myself to ask my coach for help with bar-setting. Lol.)*

Alex: NO!

Hell no, I don't think I set it high enough. Since becoming an entrepreneur my mindset has really shifted from playing small to keep me in my comfort zone, to expecting more from myself and others. I now rock a limitless mindset that has drastically changed how quickly I can manifest my dreams.

I don't often criticize Kati (she really doesn't take it well at first), but the instances where I feel it's worth it to face her wrath is when she is showing up small in our business. It seems to always surprise her and momentarily debilitate her when we get exactly what we've asked for and it requires her to do something out of her comfort zone.

One big difference between us is the way in which we react to not hitting the goals we've set. Where she tends to berate herself, I see it as an opportunity for growth and look forward to giving it another shot. It's another instance where things are not fifty/fifty, and it's in these moments I tend to carry her a little more.

Let's talk about how we measure success, because even in that there is a huge difference in how the two of us approach this concept. Kati measures success by how quickly and efficiently she can reach her goal; if she can nail a design in the first try, she considers it a complete success. If it takes her a few iterations therefore affecting the timeliness of the project, the success becomes less of a victory.

I measure success by how happy the client is with the result of my work, not just how much money I made them, but that I surpassed their expectations. I love getting phone calls out of the blue with an excited client on the other end of the line sharing that they are completely booked solid for the next quarter.

A major win for me is when we get a referral from an existing client because they've had a positive experience with us. It's because we set the bar so high that we are able to produce exceptional results that have our clients referring their contacts to us. Would we set the bar so high if relationships weren't important to us? If we were just going to deliver a one-time solution and not worry about what came next, would it be worth our while to work as hard as we do? No way! But because we want to be around for as long as our clients are in business, we go above and beyond before, during, and well after the project is complete to continue to support them and their growing business.

Even though we measure success differently, we both strive to reach lofty goals, which benefit our clients and ensure that we keep getting better in our business and our relationship.

31

Wrapping It Up

We hope we've successfully conveyed that we are partners in everything, from running a business together, to having kids together, to becoming the best possible version of ourselves together.

It's not always easy and there are definitely challenges that arise, but it's the way we choose to navigate the difficulties that makes our business and our relationship a success.

Being in a partnership does not mean a perfect fifty/fifty balance. If you go into a business partnership knowing that there will be times when you are giving 80% while your partner is only able to give 20%, there won't be any resentment and you can expect the same level of support when you aren't performing at your best.

Just because you're a twosome in your business, doesn't mean there won't be times when you need an objective third party to offer guidance and mediation. A business coach is a solid investment that'll help you set up guidelines for who is responsible for what in the business. With clearly defined roles in place, it limits the amount of conflict that can arise and helps to keep you focused on what you're the best at in the business.

While it's not always easy to turn off work and be present with each other as a couple, it's important to find ways to connect that force you to leave work in the office. Set aside breaks throughout the day that allow you to focus on something other than work, like playing a board game, cooking together, or going for a walk. Take vacations that force you to take longer periods of rest in between bouts of work; it's crazy how quickly you can forget to make time for fun in your life when you're both focusing on growing a business.

Bring a little extra patience and kindness to your work relationship because there will be more times of frustration in the long hours of working side by side. Allow your partner to nudge you out of your comfort zone and when you enter into a sparring match, don't let it escalate to a point in which you burn each other to the ground.

Being partners in everything has been our motto since day one. Growing a business together was always the dream and even in this experience, which has its ups and downs, we just keep getting better!

Star and Mark Tomlinson
The Drain Company

A couple-owned, family-operated plumbing company with the goal of franchising their system to one hundred locations in the United States.

32

Our Unique Take on Business in Our Industry

There are a lot of plumbers out there. There are a lot of drain cleaners out there. There are *not* a lot of companies that do both.

Most plumbers generally do not like to do drain cleaning. Being a drain cleaning specialist is rarely a specialty in the plumbing industry, and you would think that it would be a part of it. Historically, a drain cleaning was something that plumbers would avoid. They felt as if they could not put a high value on drain cleaning.

They *could* put a high value on plumbing. Plus, most general plumbing problems are not as dirty. Drain cleaning deals involve the sewer so there is a lot of *muck* involved. Not that plumbing does not have muck—you actually have muck in the pipes, but not as much as with sewer cleaning.

We *began* as a drain cleaning company that my grandfather founded.

In the last few years, we added general plumbing because of a necessity for our customers. They were the ones that were demanding that we offer plumbing because they did not *want* to call anyone else. We would go out on a call for a clogged drain, and while we were there, they would say that they also had a plumbing problem.

Initially, I would try and give them the name of someone to call. I referred out a *lot* of plumbing work. But repeatedly they said, "we only trust you. We don't want to call anybody else." The people that we found for them were trustworthy, honest people, but for our customers to have to call two different companies was inconvenient for them. And, at first, I didn't always know if that customer was going to come back to us.

Then we began to really crunch the numbers and we saw how much money we were giving away through the years by referring out the general plumbing business. The company evolved to meet more needs for our customers.

But our first love in the industry *is* drain clearing as opposed plumbing repair. Plumbing jobs can be unpredictable compared to drain cleaning. My grandfather used to say that "every drain can be cleared—it just takes some work." With plumbing, you can fix a leak in one place and the next weakest spot in the plumbing system of the building will leak next.

With plumbing repair, you end up chasing the leaks all around the house. With drain cleaning there are times where one may go out to clean the main sewer line and end up a few weeks later with the shower stopped up. My guys are trained to check *every* drain when we go in. We make sure that everything is draining as well as it can be.

Occasionally, we get there for a shower drain and a couple of weeks later the main line backs up. That can happen. But it does not happen as frequently as when you fix a leak. Sometimes when you fix a leak, the next thing you know is that you have a major leak. And as you chase that leak around the house, the homeowner starts to wonder what is going on (and I cannot blame them). How do you explain the charges for that? How do you explain that the possibility can occur in advance?

In the industry, we often see that plumbers are just hoping for those leaks. And if they need to clean a drain along with the job, they don't really *want* to do it. We view the industry very differently from those plumbers.

We never want to be called a lost-leader company offering a cheap drain cleaning in order to get in the door so that we can then recommend much higher plumbing costs. Other plumbers may want to go in there to look at the drain, but they don't really want to do the drain cleaning. They are there looking for the bigger repair.

When *we* go in, we want to fix everything, and we want to be able to save our customers as much money as possible by not having *to do* the major repair.

We understand that it is necessary to focus on quantity, more jobs, less time spent on the job, more efficiency. We always evaluate the house before we start just in case there are additional issues. We do not want to be short-sighted and only focus on what fits our needs for the moment; we really need to look at the power of efficiently making money and being able to expand the company with those dollars. And it is a matter of creating multiple streams (pardon the water joke there) of income for our company.

33

It's All in the Family

People always ask how *I* got involved in the plumbing industry. I grew up with it all around me as a kid because of my grandfather's drain cleaning company. It was a family affair; my grandfather and other family members all worked together. The terminology was around me all the time. I heard "stoppage" and I was unable to tune it out. Plumbing was just part of the conversation constantly. Who knew that ten years later I'd purchase the company?

My early job was to help my mom with the phones. That is how I began in the business. My grandfather, mother, and stepfather all worked together. I guess it was just natural that I would become part of it.

So, when I first bought into the company, I worked the phones. I did the calls during the day, mom did some of the nights, and then for some of the weekends we would switch off. I worked the phones from the morning to evening for four and a half years.

We did not take vacations. We did not go away. Eventually, I hired an answering service, and we finally got a break from answering the phones.

When I bought the company, Mark and I were not married but we were a couple. He was working at a brake mechanic shop with his parents—we were both part of a family business. Unfortunately, his parent's shop had to close so for the first time in his life, Mark found himself without a job.

I had recently bought into the company, and I wanted to hire Mark. My grandfather trained him along with my mom's boyfriend, and there we were, one large extended family business.

Mark is my very technical MacGyver guy. If anything breaks, he can figure out how to fix it. My man is *incredibly* mechanically adept. Although we were not exactly working side by side, he transitioned from one family business right into another.

You know, we met when I was ten years old and although things have not always been smooth, we have always been the best of friends. I was a teenager when I realized that he was, and is, the love of my life. So even when things did not go smoothly, we have always had a tight connection.

There is no one in the world that has ever meant more to me, and he reminds me every day that he feels the same way.

We work very cohesively together and support each other completely through good times and bad. No matter what circumstance we are faced with, we both just adapt and never take anything personally.

The upside to all that phone time was that I *really* got to understand my customer and understand the business. To learn more of the terminology, I would go out in the field with Mark so he could show me how to do specific things and I could conceptually understand.

I may not be able to stick the cable down the drain, but I know how it works. My grandfather always said there is no drain that cannot be unclogged. If you work at it, you can open it. With me on the phone and Mark out there doing the work, if it's taking longer, no one gets frustrated because I know why he will not give up.

Now, I am not only watching the books and the accounts, but I am the marketing director making social media work. We have hired a few people to keep an eye on it constantly. I like things that are funny and lighthearted and that make fun of humans. (Let's face it, we're pretty funny creatures!)

Mark's workday starts at seven to eight o'clock and he goes from job to job to job. He's constantly being told what to do, which would bother me. But all he says is, "Where do I go next?" That personality trait really fits the role. He is that even-keeled guy who just enjoys getting the job done right.

Our workday can be 24/7. I'm constantly looking at Yelp, making sure that we're answering our Yelp and social media reviews.

We don't relate to the term *power couple*. For the most part, people know me as the face of the company, and when Mark goes out to do the great work in the field people know we are the owners. (Some people are sad when one of our techs show up instead of Mark, because they just love talking to Mark.) We work well together and make things happen. We prefer the term *well-balanced team*.

34

The Balancing Game

I am the inside operator and Mark runs the operations in the field.

Customer service just came as a natural thing to me, I guess, because I'm a consumer and I looked at our industry as a consumer. I continually ask, "How would I like to be treated?" I am frequently surprised when I see competitors not treating their customers as they would like to be treated.

Since Mark is so good at what he does, our general rule is that I do my thing, and let him do his thing. I trust him in the field to make decisions as he sees them, and he trusts that I'm making good business choices in the office.

A challenge that we have worked to overcome is making sure to run all those individual decisions by each other. I think that I should probably run things by him more.

I'm the boss 51% of the time, although Mark and I see ourselves as equal partners. It wasn't always that way, but when he got his plumbing license, I felt it only fair to give him half.

I'm willing to be 51% as a woman-owned company, but, neither one of us has a power trip. He is good at what he does; I'm good at what I do. He lets me do what I do, and I let him do what he does. I think that having completely different roles helps us stay in our own lane.

As equal partners we push each other to want more; we also provide a sounding board and play devil's advocate. We are the Jiminy Cricket on each other's shoulders.

We have a physical office where we are most of the time. It's where we can do billing and have meetings with our technicians. But, just like most of the work world, COVID brought us home more. Although I already had an office at home as well. I like being home. There are times that I like being home and times I like being at the office. So having that extra space works well for

103

me, if I need to get away, I can. Mark, of course, is out in the field most of the time.

Mark is the man on the job; he shows up as the face of the company after they have hired us. We don't keep it any kind of a secret that he is my husband. Especially, if they met us because of my networking events. We don't shy away from letting people know that we are a family-owned and that my husband is a technician.

The only downside to people knowing that we are the owners is that we often get asked for discounts, even though we price everything for a very fair price. Emphasis on the word *fair*.

We do have *couples-only* hours. Going out to dinner we have been known to turn off our phones completely for a bit of time.

One of the ways we know that we are entrepreneurs is that there are times when we look in a mirror and say, "Yes, I am currently in workaholic mode."

There are a couple of ways we try to avoid that, and to get out of it when we are in it.

One way is to get a hobby. For us it really works. We happen to love the entire process of how wine is created from the ground through the bottle. We go to vineyards and allow ourselves to get lost in the day. We also have a friend who plays three holes of golf, then walks the rest of the course. She takes more photos than swings.

You do not have to be glued to your office seat, no matter where it is. Use technology to plug in from anywhere. It can allow flexible work hours and a way to balance your personal and professional commitments.

We think that providing for recharging is important for our employees, too. We keep reading that most people in the United States still don't take their annual leaves even when they can afford to. We encourage our employees to take those breaks, because if it's good for us, it is good for them, too.

We combine those breaks with employees a bit by making room in our work schedule to have regular team outings. They build team engagement and allow us all to know each other outside of the daily workday.

Our longest vacation together was twenty-two days. We have a good team, so it was east to get away. We have also taken a lot of seven-to-ten-day trips, though most are about four days.

And it so nice to take those breaks. Please do yourself the favor of taking breaks as regularly as possible. It just takes a bit of planning.

If we are shorthanded technician-wise, it is hard for Mark to leave, so we have to be flexible. For my half of the business, I just need a working phone and maybe access to the internet.

If you set your rules for working on vacation, you can enjoy your time and not stress out about it. At the beginning, I used to start stressing as soon as we left. I stressed out a lot because I want to make sure that we were providing excellent customer service. That is my main priority—to make sure that the customer is taken care of. If there are any glitches, we want to be sure that it is being taken care of from wherever we are.

So, wherever we go, even in Europe where the time change is greatest for us, we are still actually kind of at work. To us it is a twenty-four-hour business. However, there are times we're in areas where you can't be reached—a cruise or out somewhere away from cell service—so we are forced to relax. Hey, we're human! And it isn't brain surgery; no one is going to die. Especially, since we have an amazing team back home.

We don't have any partnership agreement and have never had a challenge in defining our partnership. We've never, honestly, ever fought over money. For us, if money is there, it's there. If it's not, it's not. That's just the way it is. We've never had money as any one of ours goals. Money just makes more things affordable.

And we are grateful for that because we know couples that work together, and they fight about money constantly. For them it's just a constant issue and I'm so grateful we don't have that.

We know we operate differently than many couples. We don't have a threshold rule; that's not us. We know other couples that do have those boundaries. You crossed the threshold—no more work time. There is always business to talk about and we are, to a certain degree, always on. But, if one of us I not in the mood to talk about something we have one agreement—we'll talk about that later.

Our agreement is to love each other first. Work together second. And deal with any challenges honestly and know that we are partners in everything, just like the title of this book.

35

Where We Go from Here

We *never* feel that the bar has been set too high!

Our vision for The Drain Company is that we will begin to franchise the brand. We have been grooming my daughter to come in and take over as we do it. My love is training so I want to be available to train our partners.

That is how our business will continue to grow through the fourth generation of growth. The vision is to sell a hundred franchises. We love the idea of the Power Hundred!

Many people have asked me "Why do you want to go through the hassle of franchising? Don't you know how hard that is going to be?" The answer is *yes*; we know it's going to be hard, but anything worth doing and having is going to have some difficult parts. We believe in the power of the family business. Our family business has provided not just a living but a life for three generations of our family now and we want other families to enjoy success as well. We want to help them build a better life, not just for this generation, but their future generations.

One of Mark's superpowers is teaching all things plumbing. One of my superpowers is organizing a plumbing business and marketing it. We are creating our standard operating procedures that will make it easy for franchise partners to quickly jumpstart their own business. We want to create a turnkey system for them, so we're identifying frequent questions, and providing them with standard responses. We will give them strategies for handling customer concerns. We will even train someone who is new to the industry.

Our motto for this project is from Dhirubhai Ambani, "If you don't build your dream, someone else will hire you to help them build theirs." We want, more than anything, to help people build their own American dream like we have been able to build ours at The Drain Company.

36

Parting Wisdom

We thought that this would be a great place for us to add our favorite inspirational quotes for success so that you can add some inspiration to your bathroom mirror. (And when it's *on* your bathroom mirror, think of The Drain Company!)

"I can't give you a sure-fire formula for success, but I can give you a formula for failure: try to please everybody all the time."
Herbert Bayard Swope

"Success is not how high you have climbed, but how you make a positive difference to the world."
Roy T. Bennett, The Light in the Heart

"Failure is the condiment that gives success its flavor."
Truman Capote

"Success is stumbling from failure to failure with no loss of enthusiasm."
Winston S. Churchill

"If A is a success in life, then A equals x plus y plus z. Work is x; y is play; and z is keeping your mouth shut."
Albert Einstein

"I'm a success today because I had a friend who believed in me and I didn't have the heart to let him down."
Abraham Lincoln

Section Two

How Other Partners Do It

We interviewed other partners to see how they balance and organize their work and relationship. You'll find author information at the end of the book starting on page 155. Here are the partners who shared their experiences.

Cindy and Stephen Crossett
Crossett Financial Services

Mary and Kirk Johnson
M&K Property Management and Peacock Print Co.

Lindsey MacNeil and Xander Calderon
LeanIn Design

Lynn and Richard Huber
LoveMyBeautyBiz.com

Hilary Blair and Dr. Robin Miller
ARTiculate: Real&Clear

Billy and Sally Green
Housecleaning Plus

Guy and Amy Grussing
Grussing Roofing, Inc.

Michael Voogd and Shelly Cook
Voogd NinjaToons

Chris and Heidi Koll
American Solutions for Business

37

Tell Us about Your Partnership

Cindy and Stephen Crossett
Cindy: I own a financial services firm where my only focus is helping my clients reaize their retirement goals. What sets me apart is that my clients are family to me, and I want what is best for them even if it means telling them things they don't want to hear, but they need to hear. The average age of my clients is twenty-five years or more my senior. Most advisors my age tend to go ten years plus or minus their age. This is a tremendous benefit to my clients; when they need me the most, when their beneficiaries need me the most, I will be there for them.

I started at the firm in 2010, and in 2020 became the owner. When my assistant unexpectedly quit, my husband and I had a conversation about him stepping in. It has become an incredible fit.

Mary and Kirk Johnson
Mary: Our business is M&K Property Management. It is a true family business that was born out of the necessity of someone needing to take over the management of my mom's rental properties after my father's passing so she could downsize and not be burdened. Living in the closest proximity, we volunteered and took over the day-to-day management of her three duplexes, one home, and after her move, her main house. From that starting point, we have since acquired income property of our own, consisting of two single-family homes plus a tri-plex. And most recently, my mother-in-law's house after her move into assisted living. Every property we manage is family-owned.

Kirk and I started dating in 2000 and have been married for fourteen years. We both have a strong commitment to each other and our relationship, and open and honest communication. Though it's not perfect, we make sure to check in with each other often about emotional health, make time to connect, and create family time. M&K Property Management is a secondary business for both of us. Kirk has a more than full time job in aerospace as a technical mechanic, and I am the owner of Peacock Print Co., a printing and promotional products provider (MaryThePrinter.com). We have deep respect and appreciation for each other and what we each bring to the relationship. I cannot stress enough that communication is the key component to keeping our relationship happy and in order.

I grew up in the rental property business. My dad was big into acquiring income property and he managed them all himself. Kirk had always wanted to get into it but didn't really know how. We both knew that we wanted a business that could take us into retirement, and that we could work together.

Lindsey MacNeil and Xander Calderon

Lindsey: I'm the founder and CEO of LeanIn Design. I help companies fix challenges for their customers, sometimes before they start. For businesses that've been around for a while, I help resolve the pain points that customers might be having with teams and workflows. The advantage for a company is that I do it in a way that increases your profit and capital—especially human and social capital.

In many ways our partnership started when we were first dating. Xander was a help-desk representative at a company that I was consulting at back in 2011. Though there were rules against dating, we obviously didn't follow those rules. He has been my go-to advisor on everything with my career ever since. I'm someone who must live by my moral code. He not only understands that, but we've achieved a state in our relationship where we help each other live our ethical ideals while keeping one another grounded.

We're yin and yang. It took us awhile to get here, but we've come to a place where we balance one another out and aim to be supportive of the other.

Lynn and Richard Huber

Richard: We are technically independent Avon representatives; as a husband-and-wife team, we sell Avon and we build a thriving team.

We provide excellent customer service in a world where most Avon (or direct salespeople even) don't take their business seriously. Our customers know we can be depended on to make sure they receive an Avon brochure every campaign, return their calls right away, deliver their orders when expected, and that we are there for the long-haul.

For our team, we provide systems to help them be more consistent, we provide training to help them be successful, and we are there to support them and help them build their business. Our team knows that we always do what is right for them and their business, not what serves our interests.

We sort of fell into an Avon business twenty years ago. The year was 2001, and the internet was just becoming mainstream. We loved to square dance, and Lynn is a geek, so she wanted to create a website for square dancing. To run a square dance calendar, Lynn needed database capabilities on the website, and that was a little expensive.

So, we were just looking for a way to pay for the website. Lynn did some research and found that Avon was promoting eRepresentatives and that you could sell Avon totally online. We thought that would be perfect and that it would help pay for our expenses.

Avon wasn't quite there though, and the whole "sell Avon online" didn't quite work yet. So, we passed out brochures at dances and got started anyway.

We weren't looking for a business. We thought we were living the perfect life.

We had dream jobs and we were making the minimum credit card payments. But we worked long hours, and Lynn commuted three hours a day to and from her job. We couldn't just take a vacation any time we wanted; we were tied down to those jobs.

It didn't take us long to see the opportunity that we had in our hands. It had never occurred to us that we could build an Avon business and live our life on our terms.

So, we thought we'd just see what would happen if we got serious. We put some real effort into it and the rest is history. It didn't take us long to become debt-free and be able to retire from our jobs.

Now we live life on our terms. We call the shots, and we decide when we are going to work.

Hilary Blair and Dr. Robin Miller

Hilary and Robin: We are an interpersonal communication consultancy working with individuals and teams desiring impact and influence. We cultivate the unique strengths and style of each individual through the techniques and discipline adapted from the performing arts. Maximizing leadership presence, we ensure voices are heard so teams are more effective, organizational cultures thrive, pitches are successful and leadership messages have true impact.

We provide laser focused heart-centered feedback, all performing arts based, and decades of teaching and coaching experience.

Before founding the business, we had taught together at the Denver Center for the Performing Arts. We decided to go off on our own for several reasons. We work well together because we are quite different but are grounded in similar values.

We have been life partners for twelve years and married for four. We co-own the business and are CEO and CFO/COO.

Billy and Sally Green

Sally: We have been in the home and office cleaning business together for over twenty years part-time and full-time for the past eleven years. I started the business, Housecleaning Plus, in 1995 right after our daughter, Amanda, was born. I've been doing it ever since. Billy had been helping me part-time and joined full-time in 2010. Many of our residential cleaning accounts are working professionals, elderly, or disabled. Our customers have become friends and our business has become a ministry of sorts. In addition to the cleaning, we help them with tech stuff, read and sort mail, fill out forms, run errands, organize closets, change lightbulbs, feed pets, etc.

We have been married for thirty-five years. I'm the dreamer; Billy is the practical one. I'm artistic and love to teach. Billy is detailed, enjoys being with people, and is a huge sports fan. We both have a great sense of humor, and we enjoy each other's company. We both love to talk so we have had some deep conversations, fits of laughter, and sometimes heated debates. I joke that I keep firing him, but he keeps showing up for work.

I started cleaning houses after getting laid off from a computer company in the early nineties. The company I worked for rebuilt computers and with the increase in technology, customers were finding it cheaper to purchase a new computer rather than build one to suit. So, my job was eliminated. My daughter was small, and I began cleaning to earn extra income. Before long I was working every day and had a waiting list.

At the time, Billy was working at a job he disliked. So, I convinced him to start working with me on weekends. One of my customers offered him a job working a couple nights a week selling hot tubs and sunroom enclosures. He left his job and joined me during the day cleaning and worked at night doing sales. Then in 2008 with the housing crash he lost that job, and we began looking for more cleaning work. We were offered a job in a fifty-five and older community cleaning and maintaining their clubhouse. We did that until Covid hit in 2020. We then added window cleaning, rug cleaning, and other home services. In addition to our commercial and residential accounts, in 2021 I started a new business helping women on their self-care journey.

Guy and Amy Grussing

Amy: We are an exterior remodeling company. It is a second-generation family-owned business and celebrating fifty years this year!

We've been married almost twenty-seven years and in business for thirteen years together. We are growing individually as well as together. We encourage each other to be and do the best!

In 2008, Guy needed help following a large hailstorm, so I started then. And later that year, Guy's dad decided to retire. So, it was a perfect time for me to step in and take over the financial affairs of the business. As Guy says, "no one better to trust with our money than Amy!

Michael Voogd and Shelly Cook

Michael: NinjaToons is an art instruction school dedicated to helping students ages six and up unleash their creative potential. We apply the structure of the martial arts with the creative arts to allow students an opportunity to explore many different disciplines in art. Focusing on *fun* art, the many classes we offer are represented as an artistic *belt*, with drawing, painting, sculpting, acting, writing, animation, comic strips, illustration, and caricature. There is no other art instruction school around like NinjaToons!

Cover and move. It's about teamwork. You never know how much someone will do for you when they are feeling appreciated. Reciprocity is the key to moving forward. *Siempre adelante*—always forward. We each have numerous jobs, roles and responsibilities, which require multitasking and communication. We support each other in the chaos of the day, by providing the assistance necessary to help each other move forward when it is needed. We also have our inner superheroes, which allow us to persevere when things get tough. These characters also have a great moral compass which help us to make the right decisions in the heat of battle. Shelly embodies Wonder Woman and Michael is Captain America. What a *team*!

Even before we were dating, Shelly was always supportive of my business and artwork. She has always been a networker, and was able to connect me with clients, which I've always been appreciative of. Now that we are working together, that desire to see me succeed has only increased. In fact, she introduced me to the idea of having a physical space for NinjaToons by tricking me to the mall to "show me something." Once there she introduced me to the mall manager to look at a few spaces. Her vision at the time was larger than what I was prepared for, but with her encouragement, she inspired me to go for it. And that's why I made her the CIO of NinjaToons, which I made official on her business cards as my chief inspiration officer. Now she helps with my events, social media posts, and networking in groups that I would not otherwise be able to enter, such as mom's social media groups.

Chris and Heidi Koll

Heidi: Chris is a distributor of print, direct mail, and promotional products. He has been in these industries for more than twenty-five years. What sets us apart is that we are independent and working for the client but part of a larger organization that provides access to unlimited resources! No job is too big or too small. Because we are independent, we can work with clients personally and create a one-stop-shop for their brand.

We work extremely well together as a team. We have so many complementary skills. For example, I'm better at time management and streamlining processes, while Chris is comfortable working with spreadsheets and calculating profit margins. Chris has stronger technical skills, but I have stronger perceptive abilities. We both are rather good at editing one another's work and we are at our best when we are brainstorming. We understand who does what best and each of us is willing to let the other person play to their strength.

We began as work partners when we were dating, Chris would bounce ideas off me and hired me to create gift baskets for clients. A year after we were married, we had a son and I became a stay-at-home mom and continued to help with ideas, projects, and of course gift baskets with homemade treats!

38

How Is Your Work Organized?

Who Does What?

Several of our couple-partners work full-time at their business with both partners in an active day-to-day role. Others have organized the partnership with both being active partners, but one having more of a public face with the other behind the scenes. And several of the partners have more than one job or business, sometimes having one member in a silent role, or both floating together from business to business.

Let's hear how they describe their roles, and how they spend their time.

Lynn and Richard Huber

Lynn is more introverted, and as such the technical-type duties are more comfortable and enjoyable for her.

Richard is more extroverted, and he enjoys working and interacting with people.

We both work together, and each provide feedback and perspective when business planning or making decisions. That works great because even though our personalities are quite different, we both have the same (or similar) beliefs, values, dreams, and goals.

And we balance each other out. Lynn helps Richard to be more consistent, while Richard helps Lynn to be more outgoing.

But it goes deeper than that. Richard works hard to take the distractions away so Lynn can focus on the business details. That means talking with a customer when the phone rings. But it also means he handles some of the household chores such as cooking and laundry to free Lynn up to do more for the business.

Each day is filled with different activities.

Lynn mostly handles the operational, computer, and technical ends of the

121

business. Her day is filled with blogging, recruiting, follow-up, creating content, marketing, and troubleshooting for both team members and customers. She runs business reports and crunches the numbers. She also runs team reports and does recognition to team members via social media and email. Then she passes that information to Richard, and he sends recognition cards from SendOutCards. She manages any online orders we get from customers and places our regular bi-weekly order with Avon.

Richard spends most of his time working with the customers. His day includes talking with customers on the phone and in-person and taking their orders.

Then he processes the order when it arrives from Avon, sorts and bags customer orders, and delivers them to the customers.

Richard sends thank you, birthday, anniversary, recognition, or other appropriate cards from SendOutCards.

We don't typically have set office hours. Most of what we do is during the day. But we do have some evening team meetings, and some of Lynn's marketing happens after we've spent our time together but before she goes to bed.

We also do breast cancer vendor events, typically twice a month at the local mall. Lynn manages and recruits vendors for the events, while Richard manages our Avon table. He decides the products that will be shown and interacts with attendees and potential customers.

Guy and Amy Grussing
Guy does the estimating and selling for projects. He manages jobs and trains new sales consultants. Amy works with marketing and finance.

On an average workday Guy is out estimating new jobs and managing those in progress and the workers. I work in the office part-time in marketing and finance. We are blessed to have a couple slower months each winter.

Billy and Sally Green
I do the invoicing and recordkeeping. When we clean houses or offices, I clean the kitchens and bathrooms, Billy takes care of the dusting and vacuuming. Billy also makes all the deposits at the bank and creates our daily and weekly schedule. He also makes many of the phone calls for new business.

We wake up and have breakfast and depending on the day, we may ride to work together. But most days we take separate cars to the same place. I like quiet on my drive in the morning and Billy enjoys sports talk radio. We have both residential and commercial cleaning accounts so our schedule changes daily and monthly.

Being a husband-wife team means that we can do some of the heavier lifting, and also attention to detail that needs to be done.

Chris and Heidi Koll
Chris handles the sales, and Heidi will help with administration, marketing, and proposals. We try to let each other use their strengths.

Work weeks are never the same, it really depends on the client's needs and our goals. One big thing Chris has taken from working with the Yuloff's is developing a strong list of goals—one for "fastest to cash" and two for "developing ideas and opportunities." Both have action items associated with them, some with hard deadlines while others are more flexible with future times. It helps to fill in those times when things are slow or if there is a change of plans.

Hilary Blair and Dr. Robin Miller
Hilary is CEO, speaker, and lead group trainer and consultant. She has an MFA in acting and thirty-five plus years of experience teaching. She does most of the visioning, curriculum and content development, networking, and most of the keynotes.

Robin is CFO/COO and is an executive coach and facilitator with a MA in music, MDiv in theology, and Ph.D in opera. Robin handles all financials and operations as well as the higher-level leadership work.

The day to day is a combination of office and team tasks, networking and relationship building, and presenting, training, or coaching. Our weeks are quite varied from multi-full day programs with multiple coaching sessions to a forty-five-minute podcast interview or a keynote.

Seasonally, it's a tad slower in August usually, but other than that it's steady.

Cindy and Stephen Crossett
I'm the financial advisor and the boss, and Stephen is my assistant and does what I need.

Every day is different which makes things exciting. I may have client meetings or webinars or be working on a client proposal. It is all driven by client need. I also have two satellite offices along with meeting at client's home or a nearby restaurant.

Lindsey MacNeil and Xander Calderon
I run it, and he's basically a silent partner.

Xander is a full-time employee with a small information technology company and I'm working on growing my business. He works more than fifty-hour weeks, primarily focused on his full-time role but also helping me as my co-pilot.

Mary and Kirk Johnson

Kirk is fix it guy. I'm money and finance. When there is a vacancy, we divide up the work between what Kirk will be taking care of and what I'll be contracting out. I usually will hire, meet and oversee all the outside workers, and Kirk will be the final inspector. I handle listings, vetting, and leasing. We both meet the prospective tenants prior to a lease signing—a must in my book. Kirk handles the mortgages, and I take care of paying the smaller bills and the taxes. I tell new tenants to call Kirk if something breaks or needs fixing, and to call me if they have a financial issue.

When things are going well, we may not have day to day work in the property business. When there are repairs or vacancies, we still need to fit the work around our other jobs. So, it's a true cooperative effort.

Michael Voogd and Shelly Cook

Initially, I wore every single hat that a small-business owner could wear. I had to make the connections, create the artwork, invoice the clients, make the phone calls, post to social media, and teach the classes. Thanks to Shelly, we can capitalize on our strengths. I focus on creating the artwork, teaching the classes, recording YouTube videos, and presenting my business to clients with studio tours. Shelly has been a tremendous help connecting me with parents, exposing me to greater client circles, and posting social media marketing updates.

We are currently in the mindset of minimizing the noise, the distractions and the physical, mental, and emotional clutter. Michael balances his structured 6 a.m. day-job with the flexibility of running NinjaToons in the late afternoon, and other commissioned projects such as illustrating children's books, and creating caricatures for clients during his off-time.

NinjaToons is open Monday through Friday from 3:00-8:00 p.m., as well as on weekends for birthday parties and other special events. During the summer we offer cartooning camps where students learn to create their own characters, comic strips, and flip books.

Physical Spaces

Our partners illustrate how many ways there are to create productive places to work. Several have commercial space. They may often have a second office at home. Several of them work from home in a variety of ways.

Commercial Office Spaces

These partners have a commercial space, often a home office as well.

Cindy and Stephen Crossett

The main office is in Cottonwood Arizona, but I also have a satellite office in Prescott Arizona and Phoenix Arizona.

We do have an office at home; sometimes it is due to a work need, sometimes to make time to do things as a couple that are not work-related. We try to keep work within the home office and not anywhere else in the house.

Hilary Blair and Dr. Robin Miller

We have an office overlooking downtown Denver. It's a gorgeous space with amazing views. We use the open space for the group programs and the smaller offices for our coaching sessions. Now we have turned it into a full-on virtual studio with two cameras, and we can stand and move around as we present. Our furloughed theatre-tech friend did the design and rework.

Our home is our second office—rather two offices. It was the classic office over the garage when we first started; now that is one personal office.

Guy and Amy Grussing

We share an office in the lower level of a building, and also have a part time bookkeeper.

Our home absolutely becomes a second office! Because of limited space in the primary office, our dining room becomes a work area. It usually gets cleaned for the weekend and before family meals.

Michael Voogd and Shelly Cook

There is no other school like NinjaToons and you can feel it before you even walk into the studio! As patrons walk by, they can look over my shoulder through the large studio windows and watch me create a step-by-step lesson, a caricature, or an illustration for my next children's book. From the moment you enter the drawing dojo, you feel a state of calm. The space was meant to feel like a dojo, with all the elements of water, plants, stone, and wood on display throughout the studio. On your left is the Zen Den where parents can hang out to read, check emails, or relax as they listen to the waterfall located in the lobby.

The main classroom is where over twenty-five students can sit as I teach from my iPad and stream the lesson onto a large seventy-five-inch flat screen TV! It's very cool and allows me to zoom in on details which I could not do previously on a white board.

At the back of the studio is where our cosplay figure drawing class takes place. There are ten art horses in a semi-circle around a stage that visiting cosplayers use to pose and model their characters. Art students take this class to develop their portfolio with gesture drawings by studying human anatomy, proportions, musculature, fabric, folds, light and shadow.

Throughout the studio I have my art displayed on the walls, pictures of the amazing cosplayers that have visited the studio, and lots of cool toys and statues to further inspire the students.

NinjaToons is located about fifteen miles from our home and I am in the process of converting the back storage room to a lounge/kitchen/recording studio.

Before renting the studio space for NinjaToons, I used a converted wall closet to stage my drawing table, computer, and art library of books. I still use this space when I'm drawing at home, but now the other side of the office is set up for Shelly's business with a desktop and storage for her supplies. Shelly needed desk space to run her business, so we are in the process of decluttering the room and making it a space conducive to productivity for us both.

Working at Home

These partners work only from home in a variety of ways. Some have multiple office spaces, some no office space at all.

Chris and Heidi Koll

For many years Chris has officed in our home. With much encouragement from Heidi to improve the *fengshui*, the office recently underwent a complete renovation. Out went the old heavy wood desk and files and in came a new repurposed custom-made desk, coffee table, and console in a soft, black matte. A leather loveseat and chair were added with new paint and carpet! It has become a sanctuary. A great place to work and grow the business!

When Covid hit it created an opportunity to covert a sunroom into an office for Heidi. A fresh new paint color, new desk, and the bright light from the large widows gives Heidi a great workspace. We work on two different levels in our home. It gives us both privacy and space.

Lindsey MacNeil and Xander Calderon

Currently, we are in an apartment, and like so many during the pandemic we work at home. Our office set-ups are in two separate rooms so we can have a true separation when needed while working.

These days anything outside the home is a second office. For his full-time job, they do still have offices as they need to support customers and their servers which requires a good deal of hardware. For my work, I end up using the park and restaurants as second offices if I just need to get out for a while.

Lynn and Richard Huber
We work pretty much exclusively from home, other than when they are doing events and such.

We each have our own offices in the house, each with whatever we need to be effective in our business duties.

Billy and Sally Green
I do most of my paperwork on my computer in the living room, on a snack tray. Invoicing and phone calls are all done on my cell phone wherever I happen to be at the time. We have no office space.

My car is my second office. I keep all my equipment in the garage and in my trunk.

Mary and Kirk Johnson
For the most part, we don't have an office. A cell phone and computer pretty much cover it. We do a lot of work at our kitchen table.

Partnership Agreements
Of our interviewed partners, not one had a formal written partnership agreement. Cindy Crossett does, however, have a suggestion for negotiating one:

My tip for negotiating an agreement would be don't be afraid to put value to what you are worth. In my previous partnership negotiation, the other party began to drag things out and wouldn't commit to any numbers. I decided to crunch some numbers and put value to my contributions. It was then that we were able to move forward. It also helps to take the emotion out of the negotiating process. At the end of the day a partnership agreement is a business contract for when things aren't going so great not when they are.

Several partners had informal agreements based upon their relationship.

Lindsey MacNeil and Xander Calderon
While we don't have a written agreement one of our unwritten rules is that

neither of us makes a risky or potentially high-cost move without agreement from the other. We trust and respect one other which means that we need to communicate about anything that can affect the other. Something that we are still working on is transparency about finances. I learned the hard way. In a past LLC that folded, I had a partner who didn't communicate to me that I could be responsible for debts I was unaware of. Thankfully, I was able to walk away without any burden back then. The laws have since changed and who knows what that would end up being today.

Michael Voogd and Shelly Cook
No, we do not have a partnership agreement in writing. Just a mutual understanding that we will help each other become the best versions of ourselves, achieve our dreams, and do it while having fun together.

Chris and Heidi Koll
We do not have anything formal. Since we consider ourselves a team and recognize each other's strengths, it helps us to negotiate on decisions.

One partnership called the question.

Hilary Blair and Dr. Robin Miller
We don't have a partnership agreement now that you mention it!
    Hmmm . . . [Editor's note: Sharyn and Hank have one for tax purposes.]

And two felt they already were covered legally. In response to the question, "Do you have a partnership agreement?" Lynn and Richard Huber said, "No. For us, it's just called marriage." Billy and Sally Green responded, "No. Just a marriage certificate."

Couplehood Marketing
A little more than half of our partners use the fact that they are also a couple in their marketing. Here are some that do not use their personal relationship in marketing the business.

Cindy and Stephen Crossett
This is still very new to us, so we haven't really invested in marketing as a couple.

Lindsey MacNeil and Xander Calderon
We don't. In our situation, Xander is more of my test audience, my alpha test subject, not an active part of the company.

Hilary Blair and Dr. Robin Miller
We have not used our couplehood for marketing.

But other partners use it in everything from a slightly nuanced way, to putting it front and center in their marketing.

Mary and Kirk Johnson
People like to rent from family-owned businesses, so I push that angle when I'm showing property.

Lynn and Richard Huber
We do promote things like "your favorite Avon couple," although many of our Avon customers like having Richard as their "Avon man."
  In recruiting, we talk about how they have us as a team to support them.

Michael Voogd and Shelly Cook
It's part of our story, and testimony for how a successful relationship should be managed. Sharing our story with other couples is a constant reminder of what keeps our relationship strong. I have featured and praised her in my social media posts and YouTube videos. And every time she hands a prospect her business card, she shares the story of how I created the caricature of her that is featured on the front of it. We are also in a networking group together, and people see us smiling and happy together, as we regularly praise each other in our social media posts.

Guy and Amy Grussing
Couplehood is only shown on the *About* section of our website. However, this is the most visited part of our page!

Chris and Heidi Koll
We are just scratching the surface with marketing our business. The Yuloffs have given Chris some great ideas on developing what we would consider a living marketing plan and calendar. It is something that we can create to gain attention, readjust if an idea doesn't work to the level we want (not fail!), and

recreate with changes in the environment. Technology is changing the way we do business and together we are working to utilize new ways to create our *sidewalk signs* for prospects to ask for more information about us and how we can help them.

39

Balance

How Do You Decide on the Balance of Power?

Cindy and Stephen Crossett
Stephen: I do what is told! For me, it is a simple as that, I am here to support my wife. I hope that it will lead to more time for use to enjoy our life outside of work.
Cindy: It wasn't much of a decision to make. I ran the business prior to him coming on board as my assistant. Also, with this being a different field from his past work, he depends on me to take the lead and guide him as to what needs to be done.

Mary and Kirk Johnson
We didn't decide. It has just organically shaped itself over the years, based on our skill sets.

Lindsey MacNeil and Xander Calderon
The dog picks. Whomever Roxy is ignoring the most is the one who must do it, whatever it is.

Lynn and Richard Huber
Richard likes to say, "Lynn is the brains and I am the brawn." I think that works well for us.

Lynn makes most of the decisions, but she typically at least runs them by Richard before finalizing them to make sure he's on board. And Richard is involved enough that he has a good perspective and ideas.

Hilary Blair and Dr. Robin Miller
The balance of power just fell into place naturally. At times segments overlap and that seems to work well.

Billy and Sally Green
I'm not sure that we did decide; we each did what we do best. Many times, he has invoiced customers and I have created our weekly schedule. We each know what needs to be done and work together.

Guy and Amy Grussing
Guy oversees the management of the company and asks for my input when he feels it is necessary. I have another business that is a priority as well for me.

Michael Voogd and Shelly Cook
As a team, we each need to understand our strengths and where we can contribute most. Communication is key so we know how to help each other. It really depends on which business we are focusing on at the time. If she needs me to run an errand, watch the kids, or support her at an event, I will do that. And on occasion, I'll need her help with running a birthday party, picking up supplies, or sending an email. Neither business is more important than the other when it's your dream. So, by having an attitude of service, you can keep your ego in check and remain humble through the growth.

Chris and Heidi Koll
We really try to share in our decision-making and rely on each other for advice. Heidi tends to make very quick decisions and Chris is methodical. Over the years it seems like there is a good balance. Sometimes a quick decision works but there are times we decide to look at all the angles before moving forward. It is a nice balance!

Office Hours Versus Couples Hours
We asked our partners about how they managed that tricky line between work and home life.

Cindy and Stephen Crossett
Our true couple hours are our days off together but is awfully hard to shut off work.

It is easy to separate office hours from couple-only hours during a regular workweek. When we are at the office it is office hours, and when we are home, it is couple-only hours. It is a little gray in coming and going to and from the office that can be both work and non-work time.

♦

Mary and Kirk Johnson
With Peacock Print Co., I can start at seven in the morning with a networking meeting or as a president of our local chamber of commerce—those meetings are frequent. We are generally able to shut it down in the evening, but we don't have official rules.

Lindsey MacNeil and Xander Calderon
If Xander is on call, it's whatever the emergency caller needs. Before the pandemic we would have date nights alone or with other couples. Since the pandemic we've had a blending of time, but we try to have moments to hours throughout the day and week where we are present with one another. We know this is something we need to work on as we both want those *couple hours*.

Lynn and Richard Huber
It is hard to shut off work because Avon has become part of our life. We do try to keep our offices as the place where we do the work, and when we are not in our offices, that is our time.

Hilary Blair and Dr. Robin Miller
We try to keep office hours for our whole team—Monday through Friday, 9 a.m. to 5 p.m.—classic, unless we have special presentations. Keeping our personal life separate has worked better at some times than others. We honor when the other needs to be *no work*. But the creep of office hours during the pandemic was particularly problematic since we didn't have the drive to and from work as a break.

Due to a key change in the team, and thus team dynamics, we are finding more time off for ourselves.

Billy and Sally Green
We don't really have set couple hours or work hours. We have worked mornings, afternoons, nights, and weekends if necessary. Many times, when we are not working, we are discussing our schedule for the next day or week, talking about customers and people we have met on the jobs. Work really doesn't get shut off.

Guy and Amy Grussing

We work all hours of the day, but make sure to take time as a couple to do fun things—walks, dinner out, and weekend trips to northern Minnesota.

Michael Voogd and Shelly Cook

Other than watching an occasional show or movie together, we really don't shut off work. We are always discussing our businesses, our pipeline, prospects, and calendar. It keeps us focused and driven to keep striving and growing our clients.

Chris and Heidi Koll

Since we have children at home, we try to spend time with them in the evening and attend all their events. There are opportunities when everyone needs their own space to allow us to work on projects or plan the next day.

Vacation

Mary and Kirk Johnson

Do we work? Not unless there's an emergency! Or, if it's a planned property hunting trip. We do have a recurring story about business while on vacation. When we're on vacation, something *always* breaks! Having go-to contractors helps a lot. A few phone calls and it can usually be handled remotely. We have put off or cancelled trips because of vacancies or renovations.

Lynn and Richard Huber

Our business allows us to go on vacation any time we want. Because of that, we have committed to the proposition that our business doesn't stop while we're on vacation.

We work to take care of as much as we can before and after the vacation, so we are freed up to enjoy our trip. And Lynn has built many systems into our business which has simplified the day-to-day management. We typically spend an hour or less every morning and every evening, while on vacation to make sure that everything is taken care of. By doing this, we can keep our business going and still enjoy traveling whenever we choose.

We once went on a two-week cruise to Hawaii. Because of the availability of the internet and the systems we have in place, our customers never even knew we were gone. We scheduled our reminders before we left. We took their orders over email, text, and voicemail, and called them back when needed. And while their delivery might have been a day or so later than usual, it was confirmed that way and they didn't even know the difference.

Many of our vacations do revolve around work though, too. We attend things like Avon conventions, MLM cruises, or MLM masterminds. So, they are more like educational trips combined with vacations.

Chris and Heidi Koll
Chris does take a laptop on any trips we take, mainly to continue to keep up on emails.

Guy and Amy Grussing
It's difficult to get away from work during the busy season. Guy has trusted workers, but he is always on call to talk to them or our customers. Winters are a better time for us to travel!

Michael Voogd and Shelly Cook
It has been a rare occasion that we have been able to vacation at all. But we have been able to escape for a few days and when we do, we really enjoy it. I think we both understand the importance of unplugging, and do not discuss our businesses when we are enjoying the new scenery and experiences. We have a few upcoming trips planned that I know we are both really looking forward to. One trip is to Hawaii which had been planned previously for two years. Unfortunately, it has been delayed due to a few unforeseen circumstances. The other trip was earned by Shelly and will be happening due to her hard work and dedication within her company.

Billy and Sally Green
We used to go on vacation every year and my parents would take over the office-cleaning jobs. But my mom was diagnosed with Alzheimer's and my dad has a heart condition, so we had to stop asking them. For the past five years, we would take long weekends or days off from work but stay at home. When we did go on vacation, I had a strict rule of *no-work talk* (but we didn't always abide by it).

Hilary Blair and Dr. Robin Miller
We have only taken a few vacations without work and that is something we are changing. Some of that has to do with our arts background (and you need to work when you have it). We just happen to have it all the time, so we keep going! And we did not grow up taking vacations. We have, up until 2020, had delightful success with travel for work and tacking on a day or two here

and there for fun. We love that! It's taken us from Seattle to Copenhagen to the Bahamas. Hilary especially gets these high-end gigs at resorts and both of us go along.

Lindsey MacNeil and Xander Calderon
I have a doozy of a vacation story. We were at a friend's wedding where Xander was a groomsman. He told me on the way there that he was still on call. While the wedding was taking place (and he was actively doing his duty as a groomsman at the front of the wedding) his phone went off for work. I answered and told his boss what was going on, it turns out that his boss didn't know about the wedding. I still give him grief for this to this day (and want his boss's phone number).

There was also the time when he took me to a dentist appointment because I had to be medicated for some serious work. When I walked out of the room in a fog and ready to go home, he was helping them fix a printer.

My bad habit, beyond having a long memory, is pulling out my iPad or notepad if a thought strikes me—while at dinner or at some event—when I really should be focusing on those we're there to spend time with.

Cindy and Stephen Crossett
While on vacation it comes down to duration; the longer the time off the greater the possibility that work will need to be done.

It is challenging not to work when on vacation especially when things need to get done and there is no one else at the office who can do it.

There was one trip that sticks out in my mind. We were camping in Zion for my birthday. Before we left, I faxed in an application for a client, and mailed the check to the investment company directly. While *en route* I got a call from one department at the investment company saying they received the check but had no paperwork. I referenced the fax number and the date I had sent it to them so they could double check. I then got a call from a different department saying that they have the paperwork, but no check. It took a lot of phone calls and explaining to get the two departments to put the paperwork and the check together so we wouldn't miss the deadline for the trade date that needed to take place. It wasn't an option to get my office to just fax in the application again. Since I *am* the office, and I was out of town with limited, at best, cellphone service. At one point I was hiking up to an overlook just so that I could get enough bars to call to get the situation taking care of.

40

Measuring Success

Our partners have varying opinions as to whether they set the bar too high for themselves (sometimes differing opinions within the partnership).

Lynn and Richard Huber
All the time! We have big goals, and we work hard. We have made some big mistakes and are right now pushing ourselves to make up for one mistake that we made when we walked away from our Avon business to try another one. And so, sometimes it seems we can't build fast enough to recover the ground we lost.

While we have a high bar, we also don't beat ourselves up for not reaching those high goals if that happens. We believe that if we reach high, we will go much higher than if we set sensible goals. And so, if we don't exactly meet the goals we set, we make note of what we did accomplish and determine what we can do to make it next time.

Cindy and Stephen Crossett
Cindy: Yes, I set the bar extremely high for myself.
Stephen: Yes, I also set the bar very high for myself, but I have come to accept my limitations. I can't do everything, and it is ok to ask for help.

Hilary Blair and Dr. Robin Miller
In measuring success, we definitely set the bar too high. We've worked hard on celebrating all wins and realizing that a ten-year anniversary of our business is a great celebration as well! We just are not where we want or know we can be.

Michael Voogd and Shelly Cook

The song "Never Enough" is from one of our favorite movies *The Greatest Showman*. Some people have specific goals when it comes to financial goals, while others may have a different definition of success. For me, financial security is important because I have spent too many restless nights living on the edge. But freedom is another measurement of success. I would like to have the freedom to travel and create while still providing for my family and our future. There is nothing wrong with having big dreams and they can be achieved incrementally. Set one goal, and once you reach the top of that mountain, set another goal and climb that mountain. People like us need something to strive for as we continue to improve ourselves and influence those around us. It's been said that the greater danger is not that we set the bar too high and never achieved it, but that we set the bar too low and never reached our fullest potential.

Chris and Heidi Koll

We both are spending more time with positive affirmations and trying to develop more positive energy. When it comes to our success, we are realistic with our goals. If anything, in the past we may have settled for less with old thoughts and actions.

Guy and Amy Grussing

No, we always want our clients to have exceptional quality and service that exceeds their expectations.

Billy and Sally Green

We should have set the bar higher. Although we have done well financially, the job we do is physically exhausting, and we decided early on not to scale our business. We kept it small because we wanted to give our customers the best care and knew we would be able to provide that. Hiring others, we had no guarantee they would do the job as we did.

Mary and Kirk Johnson

Absolutely not.

Lindsey MacNeil and Xander Calderon

Xander believes I set the expectations too quickly, like planning for a marathon when really, it's a ten-meter sprint. I believe he doesn't set his goals high enough as to me he highly undervalues his abilities.

The Endgame

When asked what our partners hope for as an ending to their business and how they would like to leave, their responses fell mostly into three categories: retiring, hoping it will stay in the family and their children will take it over, or never leaving it.

Hilary Blair and Dr. Robin Miller

Our endgame has been shifting a bit, but we envision a retreat center and continued coaching for us. We will leave the business by selling or leaving it to the best team member. But this is still in the re-visioning phase.

Cindy and Stephen Crossett

My hope is that many years from now we can retire from the practice knowing that whoever acquires my practice treats my clients like I treat them. My clients are family to me.

Lindsey MacNeil and Xander Calderon

We will leave it from an economic perspective as an international, well respected and profitable firm that helps craft sustainable human focused solutions. From a social perspective, with a wealth of friends and acquaintances we can stay connected to and party with wherever we are.

Billy and Sally Green

This business was created out of necessity. I really didn't have an endgame when I started it. I just wanted to pay the bills. But over the years it has grown on us. We have some amazing customers, and we really enjoy working together. Our hope is to retire in a few years and be able to find another cleaning company to recommend to our customers.

Chris and Heidi Koll

We have teenagers so we hope to continue with our business well into the future. Perhaps one will choose a career with our business. If the time comes, our relationship with American will allow us to sell it.

Mary and Kirk Johnson

We are hoping this will be our income in retirement and beyond. Our intent would be to pass it on to our heirs and keep it in the family.

Guy and Amy Grussing
Our goal is for our son and daughter to someday take over the business and operations.

Michael Voogd and Shelly Cook
Both our businesses are still young, so there is still much growth ahead of us. As an artist, I will always be creating, so I don't think I'll ever leave my business. But I do have hopes to franchise the school and merchandise the brand to help create multiple revenue streams, so that I can step back from some of the day-to-day operations and focus just on creating. My hope would be to remain creative and less administrative in the future.

Lynn and Richard Huber
Our endgame is to be mostly selling online and building a strong residual income. We will probably never leave the business if we can build it to where we can keep it going with minimal effort.

Section Three

Thirty Tips for a Happy Business Relationship

Hank had always told Sharyn that, "We are trained as business coaches. We have certificates in neuro linguistic programming and a bunch of other disciplines that help us be the most effective coaches. We are not relationship coaches."

Uh huh. Sure. Let's see *you* go work with a lot of partners in everything and not have relationship challenges pop up from time to time. So as a nod to that part of our business, we added this chapter on business relationship tips.

There are thirty because this book was published on our thirtieth wedding anniversary. We opened this chapter up to our other authors (and a friend) for their tips.

From Amy Grussing (GrussingRoofing.com)

1. Set boundaries—*no* talking business or finances after 8:00 p.m. or earlier!
2. Find time each day to connect and enjoy each other. Just be! Go for a walk, have a cup of tea or coffee and enjoy each other—no work conversation!
3. Look to bring out the best in each other. Compliment and say thank you for one to three things your partner did that day.

From Judy Cunningham (OpenDoorWorldMinistries.com and Travorium.com/80110)

4. Even though you are a couple you must remember you have individual personalities and usually opposites attract. Don't sweat the small stuff. Let your gifts determine what role you will play and stay in your lane. Live life to the fullest, love on each other like it's no tomorrow, because one day it won't be.

From Kati and Alex Pauls (KPDesign.CA)

5. *Walk it out*—make time to walk with each other every day, especially if you're feeling tense or stressed about a work situation. When you find yourself in a situation where things are getting heated

(not in a good way) between you and your partner, pull the hand-brake on the dispute and take it outside . . . for a walk. You'll find that getting outside into fresh air, moving your body so the energy starts circulating, and not having to look directly at each other, will allow you to talk more rationally through the situation. By the time you're done your walk you'll more than likely have gotten past the block and you'll both feel better and ready to jump back into work.

6. *Celebrate every win*—it's easy to celebrate the gigantic wins in your business with your partner, but what about the little wins? Maybe you set a goal to follow up with ten clients in one day, and at 4:59 p.m. you finish your tenth call. Celebrate! If you're not physically with your partner, shoot them a text and get the happy emojis going. If you are working in the same space together, leave them a note after they've left telling them how much they rock! Being an entrepreneur takes grit and gumption, and you are bound to have bad days and hard times when you're bickering a bit more than usual. So, if you start celebrating all the wins, no matter how little, and let each other know how good of a job they're doing, the good times will outweigh the bad times!

7. *It's never fifty-fifty*—there's no such thing as a perfectly even relationship. There will always be one partner that gives a little more while the other struggles until the roles reverse. If you go into a business relationship knowing that you'll be expected to carry your partner from time-to-time and that you'll receive the same support when you need it, something called grace enters the arena. Grace allows you to show up with compassion at work so you can run your business in tandem without skipping a beat. Grace doesn't leave room for resentment because stepping up for your partner allows them to do the same for you. For grace to show up, you must be able to communicate openly with each other. If you're struggling, tell your partner right away, don't wait for them to play the mind-reading game—no one wins at that game. Communicating clearly and in a timely fashion shows respect for yourself (you're giving them a heads up before you succumb to your unchecked emotions).

From Hillary Blair (Articulaterc.com)

8. *Office hours are so useful*—if our conversation veers into business not during work hours we can pipe up with "sorry closed for biz right now."

9. *Apologies, ownership, and laughing stuff off*—wow, we can get intense with two strongly opinionated people who are *right*!

10. *Gratitude*—it's so easy to get caught up in where we want to go—simply celebrating all wins, no matter the size, and listing the gratitude regularly!

From Bill and Sally Green (TheSelfCareRockstar.com)

11. *Text each other.* Many times, we will be in the same room working together and he will send me a text with a pic of the cat and say, "hey, did you see what this guy did this morning?" Or "did you see who called today?"

12. *Use humor, have fun with each other.* Find ways to make each other smile or laugh.

13. *We have separate hobbies* but also enjoy doing things together. He likes baseball games and sports, I like painting and art. We both enjoy going to dinner with friends and working on our business goals together. Give each other the space to enjoy the things the other partner doesn't.

From Lynn and Richard Huber (LoveMyBeautyBiz.com)

14. *Have clearly defined roles* where duties are allocated based on the strengths and preferences of each person. But don't be afraid to step in when the other needs help.

15. *Make it a point to listen to each other.* Even if you don't agree, understand that you are a partnership where each person has input and perspective towards the final decisions.

16. *Set goals together.* This way you both know what you want from your business, and what you're aiming to reach. This helps eliminate conflict because you're both working towards the same goals.

17. *Stay in your lane.* And when it comes to business, all the lanes are open. If you use your turn signals, others will make room for you. The entire road is yours. That brings us to . . .

18. It's not about finding the person you want to share one life with. It's about finding the person you want to live *your* life with, like two separate lanes going in the same direction.

19. *We each back up the other.* There ain't no one who can mess with my woman without hearing from me. And they are going to hear it really loud and really proud. And no one has had my back like Sharyn. She is fierce and I love her for that.

20. Before we were married, we went for couples counseling. One of our challenges was that we would get in arguments because the other person did not answer our questions. The thing is, we did not answer because we . . . get this . . . did not *hear* the other person. How can you answer a question that you did not hear? So here was the rule that we were given, that we have used for over three decades together: If you ask a question and do not get an answer, assume you were not heard. If you are *asked* a question and you need to put together your thoughts, you simply say "thinking." The other person knows they were heard. If you are asked a question and you *have* an answer right away, then answer it.

21. If one of us cooks, the other one cleans up.

22. *Never* come home with a cat without at least texting first.

23. We no longer accept clients when either of us sees a *red flag*. This is a no-discussion rule, but we have never disagreed. We have both felt that a client was a border line red flag at some point . . . and have found that whenever we go against this rule, it is not good for our relationship.

24. *Take time for yourselves.* If you are partners, but not in a relationship, then you must take time away from each other. If you are a couple,

146

you must each, still take time for yourself. Now, as part of this rule, you must also take time off together away from everything else going on.

25. *Always continue to build trust.* Never take advantage of people, businesses, suppliers, or clients. Make sure that they would never have reason to think that you would. It's the quickest way to ruin a relationship and build a bad reputation that can harm your personal relationship, too. The key to building trust is being honest. When you are willing to forego your own interests to help someone else, they know they can rely on you. Do the right thing and be dependable, and you'll see your personal relationship and your business relationships grow stronger.

26. *It's okay to show your vulnerability.* We are human and sometimes that means sharing and supporting people through difficulty, challenge, and change. Showing your vulnerability is part of your authenticity. One word of caution: this is best shared with a select few rather than more publicly. Use good judgment here.

27. We learned from Kody Bateman that "appreciation wins out over self-promotion every single time." Failure to show appreciation is the number one reason an employee will leave your company, and it is definitely the top reason that a relationship can end. Everybody wants to know that their contributions are acknowledged and appreciated. It's too easy to forget to thank someone who shares a business lead or goes out of their way to help you solve a problem. Make a conscious effort to show gratitude for things that others do for you, and that your partner in everything does for you, and they'll be more likely to help you in the future.

28. We understand that we are the best versions of ourselves because we have each other as our biggest cheerleader. We are blessed to have the other to pick us up when we are down.

The pandemic gave us two more rules for our relationship:
29. The first, which Sharyn coined in 2020 is "Get comfortable with being uncomfortable." That rule serves us well when it comes to doing new things.

30. The second, which grew out of the first rule is "We do *nothing* which does not give us joy."

And since we are such believers in business coaches giving bonus content:

None of these rules are set in stone.

If you both agree, you don't really need a rule.

They are only relevant if you need a boundary.

For example, we heard early on that we should have a *threshold rule*. That's when you don't do business talk once you cross the threshold. Which threshold depends on you. Could be the office, could be the bedroom. The thing is, this isn't an issue for us. Our lives are fluid. We might be talking business one minute, and then switch to talking about a family member. You only need the threshold rule if one of you needs it. Since we agree that we don't need it, we don't have it.

As we are going to print, Sharyn came up with this statement: We were not looking for someone to grow old with. Our secret is that we each found someone to keep being kids with!

Epilogue

The Wheelbarrow and the Gold Coins

A few years ago, we were fortunate enough to be speaking on stage at the same event as Brian Tracy (yes, that Brian Tracy! Wait, you don't know who Brian Tracy is? Please look him up . . . your future self will thank you!). Of the dozen or so speakers, we were the only couple speakers. This was one of over two hundred days a year when Brian was on stage, teaching sales and speaking, and Hank must have taken a dozen pages of notes. He was in active learning mode because "if you are not learning, you are not earning."

After the morning session, the speakers got to have lunch with Brian. We thought that this was going to be an even *better* opportunity to learn from Brian Tracy up close. We got to the restaurant in the hotel and made sure we would be at the same table as him. We had questions at the ready. During the salad course, we noticed something. Brian was asking the other people at the table questions. *and* . . . he was taking notes, capturing what he would tell us later when we asked questions—golden nuggets.

After lunch, all 350 of us, guests and speakers, were back in the second-floor ballroom. But as we got started, we began to hear noise coming up from the pool area one floor below. There was an end of summer party going on. And it was loud. As I sat in the second row, looking up at Brian Tracy, I thought if anyone had earned the right to go ballistic (you know, "I can't work in situations like this" kind of ballistic) it would be Brian. But then, he walked to the front of the stage, leaned toward us as if sharing a secret, and said something that would forever change how I act when we are on stage. He had just given me a *forever golden nugget*.

So, imagine this: You wake up super early on a beautiful spring Sunday morning. Those mornings somehow seem magical, right? You make your coffee and decide to pour it into a travel mug to take a bit of a drive. You point your car towards the mountains and enjoy the fresh breeze on your arm and the left side of your face. The sun's just coming up, so the breeze is still a little cool. It doesn't take you long to arrive at the base of your closest mountain. You drive just little bit higher, and you come to a trail head. The sign says there are caves. Caves are always fun to explore, right?

You lean against the car, feeling the warmth of the engine on your rear, and finish the last of your coffee. You lock up the car and walk a bit along the trail. It isn't long before you find the first cave entrance. You notice something glistening along the floor of the cave. Using the flashlight feature of your smartphone, you shine it in front of you and notice the ground is layered with gold coins. Holy cow! You look around to see if anyone is watching, which, of course, no one is. You quickly gather as many of the coins as you can carry in your shirt, but there are so many more. You take off your shoes and fill your socks with coins. You carry all the coins back to your car, knowing that there are more in the cave.

"If only," you think, "I had a shovel and a wheelbarrow." Of course, you could drive the ninety minutes to a big box store and buy them. But how much do those cost? You decide, in the end, to be happy with the coins you have and head back down the hill, down to where you're comfortable. Down to the comfort of your home.

This is how we find that many entrepreneurs feel about coaching: instead of focusing on the golden nuggets, they are worried about the cost of the shovel and wheelbarrow. Instead of investing in their business, they are busy just trying to do more of what they were taught to do.

But that's not you, right? You look at business coaching as a partner-in-everything knowing you could have called them to meet you at the cave with the necessary tools.

We know that because you are committed to growing your business by investing time and money to reach your dreams. We would like to give you a free boost, a wheelbarrow to load up a new marketing plan. We invite you and your partner-in-everything to join us at The Small Business Breakthrough Bootcamp! And after bootcamp, you won't just go back down the hill to where it's comfortable. Not you. You will use everything you learn to build your business bigger and better. Sign up at PlanYourMarketing.com.

We look forward to welcoming you and helping you in every way we can! We'll fill your wheelbarrow with lots of golden nuggets. Let's get started at www.HowToGetThereFaster.com.

Author Information

Hank and Sharyn Yuloff
Yuloff Creative Marketing Solutions
www.YuloffCreative.com

As a married couple and as small business coaches, Hank and Sharyn Yuloff are passionate about helping entrepreneurs achieve their dreams. They have dedicated themselves to give clients the personal, customized attention that was lacking in the marketplace. That drove them to create the coaching program they wish they had found for themselves. They have been called "your champions of excellence and the enemies of average."

The Yuloffs approach marketing your small business from incredibly unique perspectives. Hank has a more than thirty-five-year background in advertising, public relations, and economics that began with him getting degrees in those subjects from San Diego State University. He has been a consistent top producer in the promotional products, direct mail, and online industries.

Sharyn is an online marketing expert with over twenty years of human resources and business organizational experience. For more than a decade, they have morphed their company into a complete boutique marketing services firm, offering traditional and online marketing programs that support small business owners like you. Each year, their company, Yuloff Creative Marketing Solutions, puts on several Small Business Breakthrough Bootcamp intensives for small business owners as well as working *two-on-you* with firms around the country. They have authored six best-selling business books and have more scheduled. In addition, the couple have hosted over three hundred episodes of a podcast called The Marketing Checklist and appear in an entrepreneurial video series with Brian Tracy filmed in 2016. At the end of 2017, the Yuloffs were voted "America's #1 Small Business Coaching Team."

They are extremely excited to have a new Do-It-Yourself with Coaching group coaching program—The Company Marketing Plan (CompanyMarketingPlan.com), which is available for all entrepreneurs that includes over seventy hours of private and group coaching.

What are the Yuloff Creative small business coaching programs all about? Here is a story that should explain them:

When Dorothy hit town in Oz, the first thing she had to figure out was how to not get blamed for that dead witch under her house. Since that witch's sister made Dorothy a target market of one, Miss Gale had to take a yellow brick escape path that brought her exactly to the person who could help her.

So, you could be wondering, in this story are we making you Dorothy? Is

Yuloff Creative the path? Is the Wizard your target market?

That would be too easy.

Your *competitors* are wearing the black and white striped socks, your business is the house, and we are your tornado landing you perfectly on top.

The rest is just a fairy tale.

We invite you to see how your tornado works.

This book will take you over the rainbow and teach you to avoid the flying monkeys that want to steal your dog . . . uh, we mean sales. And just like Dorothy, with the Yuloff Creative coaching programs it costs you truly little to get to the Emerald City.

Kati and Alex Pauls
KP Design
KPDesign.ca

Many people find it difficult to fathom going into business with their spouse and often marvel at couples who are partners in everything. Kati and Alex Pauls are one of those couples who have intertwined their personal and business lives and still really like each other at the end of the day! They met when they were fifteen and have been married for twenty-two years. Kati and Alex are marketing tech strategists and creatives at KP Design, a digital design agency that offers entrepreneurs a full range of custom solutions to elevate their brand so they can make more money. Since joining forces, they have doubled their business during a pandemic year and are set to double again by the end of 2021.

Star and Mark Tomlinson
The Drain Company
www.thedrainco.com

A couple-owned, family-operated, multi-generation plumbing company with the goal of franchising their system to one hundred locations in the United States.

Cindy and Stephen Crossett
Crossett Financial Services
CrossettFinancial.com

Cindy Crossett, owner of Crossett Financial Services, has been assisting investors for over ten years. Starting with a background in banking and accounting, she joined Geromino Financial in 2010, rising to partner status in 2015, and in 2020 to owner.

Cindy holds four Financial Industry Regulatory Authority (FINRA) licenses: Series 6, 7, 63, and 65, allowing her to manage money in a variety of platforms. Additionally, she has obtained her RICP (Retirement Income Certified Professional) designation. Cindy is a licensed life, health, long-term care, fixed and variable annuities insurance agent. What this means for you, the investor, is that she can provide you with an overall financial plan. Her natural ability to strategically plan is evident in her client's financial successes. The desire to assure clients that retirement is an achievable goal is deeply important to Cindy and will hopefully be apparent to you as well.

Cindy and Stephen appreciate the outdoor life Arizona has to offer along with heading out in their RV to go camping and visit National Parks. On weekends they enjoy hiking and spending time with their two cats and four dogs.

Mary and Kirk Johnson
M&K Property Management (as well as Peacock Print Co.)
PeacockPrintCo.com

Mary was born and raised in Tujunga, California and Kirk was born and raised in La Canada, California. They have stayed in their hometowns and currently reside in Sunland, California. They have two adult children, a daughter in Oxnard and a son in Costa Mesa from Mary's previous marriage. Living at home are Kirk's boys Zachary, twenty and Matthew, sixteen. Mary is busy growing her new business Peacock Print Co. and Kirk stays busy with work and gardening and renovations on their home. For recreation, they love camping trips, spending time with their granddaughters, wine tasting, cooking, and entertaining.

Lindsey MacNeil and Xander Calderon
LeanIn Design
https://leanindesign.com

A nerd and a dork have a conversation over sake and the rest is history. The nerd can be full of herself while the dork can be way too accommodating. We have been parents of three wonderful fur babies and are a support system for a few ornery relatives, lonely neighbors, and neglected spirits in the neighborhood.

Lynn & Richard Huber
LoveMyBeautyBiz.com

Most of what we do revolves around helping people live a better life and get *unstuck*. We are having an amazing time with our Avon business. We are making history and changing lives. And *Avon* has totally changed *our* lives!

As professional team leaders, we serve as mentors; teaching people how to increase their net worth by growing, cultivating, and nurturing their network, which empowers them to fulfill their biggest and most incredible dreams—whatever they choose that to be!

Just imagine the possibilities. Let's connect and explore them together!

Hilary Blair and Robin A. Miller, Ph.D.
ARTiculate: Real and Clear
WWW. ARTiculaterc.com

Hilary Blair and Dr. Robin Miller co-own ARTiculate: Real and Clear. They coach corporate teams and individuals to elevate presence, communication, and connection. ARTiculate clients include AWS, Lumen, ACLU, and MD Anderson.

Hilary is a professional communication coach with years of experience as a voice over and stage actor. She has been coaching, training, and facilitating for more than thirty-five years. She guides and challenges others to communicate more powerfully. These include the enthusiastic and reluctant alike.

Dr. Robin Miller is an energized executive coach whose primary purpose is to support others to be more adaptable and embrace the shifts needed to connect to their teams and their clients. Her insight is that the most difficult leaders and employees usually have the hugest heart without the know-how to share it.

Sally and Billy Green
Housecleaning Plus
The cleaning business is mainly word of mouth.
Website for the new business: TheSelfCareRockstar.com

Sally and Billy have owned Housecleaning Plus since 1994. They offer both residential and commercial cleaning in the Connecticut area. In addition to the cleaning, they also offer home organizing, window and rug cleaning, and other home care services. Sally has recently started a new business called "The Self Care Rockstar" where she helps women on their self-care journey. Sally is an international bestselling author with the books *1 Habit for Entrepreneurial Success* and *1 Habit to Thrive in a Post-Covid World*.

Guy & Amy Grussing
Grussing Roofing, Inc.
www.grussingroofing.com

Grussing Roofing is an exterior remodeling company. This second-generation family-owned business celebrates fifty years this year.

Michael "the ArtNinja" and Shelly Cook, CIO (Chief Inspiration Officer)
Voogd NinjaToons
www.NinjaToons.com

The ArtNinja (aka. Michael Voogd) is a local Ventura County resident with an Associate Degree in Art from Moorpark College. Studying at the California Art Institute in Thousand Oaks, California, Michael brings his passion for teaching, drawing and cartoons to NinjaToons. Michael specializes in cartoons, animation, caricatures, illustration, and comic strips. For the past ten years, he has taught art enrichment programs at numerous homeschools and after-school programs, and now students of all ages can benefit from his fun and educational instruction inside the Drawing Dojo at NinjaToons located in the Simi Valley Town Center.

Chris & Heidi Koll
American Solutions for Business
AmericanPrintPromo.com

Combined Chris and Heidi have forty years of industry experience in sales and customer service.

They are a distributor of print, direct mail, and promotional products, and apparel. As an independent representative of American they believe in proactive, customer-driven business relationships. But as part of a large co-operative, they have access to unlimited vendors for solutions in print, promo, and logistics to create the perfect solution for clients.

"It All Starts with an Elevator"
A Bonus Marketing Chapter for Entrepreneurs
Who Are Partners In Everything

If you have read our other books and attended our events, you know we are huge fans of giving bonus material. Here is your bonus content for this book!

We were about to speak to 150 business owners about social media and the best way to build your business. As I got dressed, I needed to pick a tie. A tie that would somewhat match with Sharyn's maroon shirt. From the bottom of the stack, a tie that I had not worn in years spoke to me.

"Wear me."

Wear you?

"Yes, if you wear me, I promise something great will happen."

Okay, I believe in ties, and they have never lied to me so I grabbed it and *goodness*, it was a tie with Mickey Mouse on it that says "It All Started with a Mouse."

It all started with a mouse. I thought about that for a bit. Walt Disney had a mouse with a different name. He changed it to Mickey. And drawings became cartoons. And that turned into one of the most popular brands in the world.

That made me think of something else.

Years ago, Sharyn and I were selected to participate in a group called the New Leaders Project where up and coming entrepreneurs were taught what it is like to be a business leader in your community. We met lots of other businesspeople our age, and lots of leaders in positions we aspired to reach.

One of them was retired Los Angeles City Councilman, Marvin Braude. Never heard of him? That's okay. What you must know about Mr. Braude is that it is because of him that you can eat in a restaurant and almost everywhere else without being disturbed by nasty cigarette smoke. He spoke to our group and related this story.

One day, Councilman Braude was in a downtown Los Angeles elevator with a pregnant woman and several other people who were all smoking. She coughed and Braude thought, there really should be a law that would prevent people from being forced to inhale smoke. Then he thought "I am an LA City Councilman. I can write that law."

He did and it spread from there. Soon, there were laws establishing non-smoking areas and finally, the only "Smoking Area" for Los Angeles was Las Vegas.

As Mr. Braude was speaking to us, he said that his message was simple. You can have a huge goal. But sometimes, what you need to do is start small. You can start with an elevator.

Let's talk about your elevator.

As partners in business, do you have an elevator? Do you have goals? A project you need to start? How about a project you need to finish? What ideas do you have that you have not acted upon? When are you getting started? We ask these questions to our private and group coaching clients all the time.

Do you have some goals where you have not taken a first step towards? Is it because they are so large that you are frozen by inaction? We have all heard the expression, "a journey of a thousand miles starts with a single step." It is supposed to tell us to just take that first step. Which is easy, but not when we keep looking waaaaaaaay down the road a thousand miles.

We have several goals and continually add to our list. You are holding one of them now.

This one came during a break in a mastermind session when I had a conversation with Dan Janel. Dan's business is helping first time authors go from idea to publication of their first book. He told me that "I read your book *The Marketing Checklist 2* last night and I think that you and Sharyn should write a book about couples who work together."

That was a lightbulb moment and twenty-four hours later, Sharyn and I came up with a title, a rough cover design, bought the URL, and created a list of questions that we would need to answer as chapters. Our first steps were taken, but there were many more.

Our first decision was who to include in the book. We thought we would need to find between eight and fifteen couples who want to be part of the book (we thought that it would be better to have several points of view) and are willing to invest in becoming best-selling authors. Alternatively, we could write the entire book ourselves. We decided to look for couples, and we allowed it to get us stuck for years.

We also needed to find a teeter-totter for the front cover photo. Of course, there was always the idea of hiring a graphic artist to draw us.

Another project we have is a book about how the laws of physics can be used to describe how to market your business. For that book, we are waiting for our co-author, Randy Gold, to write the physics part. Then we will write the marketing laws that tie in. For example, the 3rd Law of Thermodynamics states that (roughly, remember, I am not writing that part) a body in motion will stay in motion until acted upon by an outside force. The marketing equivalents? Your marketing is going to continue to suck until you do something to change it. Well, it may end up more gracefully than that.

Then there are two more books in The Marketing Checklist series. One will be a third marketing tips book, and the other is a sales tip book which came out in 2019. In fact, a version of this chapter became the first chapter for that book.

Each of the things on our list has a checklist of things that we need to do in order for them to be completed.

For your goals you need to do the same thing. Write down your goals so that you can know at any moment, how far along you are in your journey and you can become neither overwhelmed nor overconfident that the project will be completed. I used to laugh at writing down goals until I did it and saw that it works. The story of *The Marketing Checklist for Sales* follows my being coached through the writing of a timeline for completing that book. Ask me about it.

This list-making is especially important for the products you are selling. It is so important to checklist your process and make it easy to follow up and follow through. Your clients can also benefit from your checklist because they can follow along and realize that you are not there to get paid but are there to assist them in their business and their lives. Our clients benefit because we keep a checklist for every one of them and they become the basis for our private coaching calls.

Remember this most important of sales rules: 99.999% of people in the world do not want to write you a check. The good news is that .001% would keep you terribly busy. Your job as a salesperson, or as the owners of your company looking for new clients, is to solve their problems. If you can take away your client's pain, you will receive their support and their money.

Sales is not about you. It is about them. This book has not been about us. It is about helping you. You can say you care, but until you demonstrate it, the sales will not happen.

All you must do is help your clients ride their elevator without being disturbed by cigarette smoke.

Do you want help in finding your elevator, or helping your clients find theirs? Let's have a conversation. Go to www.HowToGetThereFaster.com and after you answer a few easy questions, you can choose a time in our calendar that is best for you.

I end this with a quote from Zig Zigler who said,

"There really is no satisfaction quite like helping someone else along life's highway. This is true, whether the person genuinely appreciates what you've done or even comments on it, though that obviously would be the desired result. There is something inside of all of us that leads us to feel that we are being our best self when we do something for others. The old Biblical quotation that "he who would be the greatest among you must become the servant of all," is true. Give helping others a try and I'll see you at the top!"

DING

Your elevator doors have opened. It's time for you to rise to the top. All you have to do is step in and want us to help you. Will you let us?

Want More Training?
What if it was FREE?

No More Business Blinders

**Getting You
Focused for
Your Success**

The Small Business/
BREAKTHROUGH
BOOTCAMP

Hank and Sharyn Yuloff
*share their proven secrets on how to
create your own successful marketing plan...*
**And they're in person to coach you.
And for YOU, it's FREE!**

All the info and register
for your free ticket at
PlanYourMarketing.com

Seating is limited. YCMS reserves the right to cancel this offer at any time.

Other Books by Naked Book Publishing

49 Stupid Things People Do with Business Cards . . .
And How to Fix Them

The Marketing Checklist
80 Simple Ways to Master Your Marketing

The Marketing Checklist 2
49 More Simple Ways to Master Your Marketing

The Marketing Checklist for Social Media Marketing
The Hows and Whys of Social Media

The Marketing Checklist for Human Resources
*The Right Way to Hire, Cultivate, and Terminate Employees,
All While Improving Your Marketing*

The Marketing Checklist for Sales
49 Easy Ways to Improve Your Sales for Professionals

And more in the pipeline as well!

The MARKETING CHECKL✓ST

"Share This Book Series"

www.ingramcontent.com/pod-product-compliance
Lightning Source LLC
Chambersburg PA
CBHW060555200326
41521CB00007B/581